Why bother?

Why bother?

Getting a life in a locked-down land

Sam Smith

FERAL
HOUSE

ISBN 0-922915-72-5

Feral House
P.O. Box 13067
Los Angeles, CA 90013

Design by Linda Hayashi

10 9 8 7 6 5 4 3 2 1

To Sally Denton,
Roger Morris, and
Russell Mokhiber.
Because they bothered,
this book was published.

Contents

INTRODUCTION

LET'S TURN OFF THE TELEVISION, STEP INTO THE SUNLIGHT, AND COUNT THE BODIES.

As we were watching inside, the non-virtual continued at its own pace and on its own path, indifferent to our indifference, unamused by our ironic detachment, unsympathetic to our political impotence, unmoved by our carefully selected apparel, unfrightened by our nihilism, unimpressed by our braggadocio, unaware of our pain. Evolution and entropy remained outside the cocoon of complacent images, refusing to be hurried or delayed, declining to cut to the chase, unwilling to reveal either ending or meaning.

We shade our eyes and scan the decay. We know that this place, this country, this planet, is not the same as the last time we looked. There are more bodies. And fewer other things: choices, unlocked doors, democracy, satisfying jobs, reality, unplanned moments, space, clean water, a species of frog whose name we forget, community, and the trusting, trustworthy smile of a stranger.

Someone has been careless, cruel, greedy, stupid. But it wasn't us, was it? We were inside, just watching. It all happened without us — by the hand of forces we can't see, understand, or control. We can always go in again and zap ourselves back to a place where the riots and tornadoes and wars are never larger than 27 inches on the diagonal. We can do nothing out here. Why bother?

Why bother? Only to be alive. Only to be real, to be made not just of what we acquire or do under instruction, but of what we think and do of our own free will. Only, Winston Churchill said, to fight while there is still a small chance so we don't have to fight when there is none. Only to climb the rock face of risk and doubt in order to engage in the most extreme sport of all — that of being a free and conscious human. Free and conscious even in a society that seems determined to reduce our lives to a barren pair of mandatory functions: consumption and compliance.

What safety we have, the privilege of the cocoon, comes from those who, at much greater danger and with far less chance or choice, climbed that wall, insisted on being human, fought despair, suppressed fear, and denied themselves the illusion of detachment. Some were only a generation or two away and carried our name, some were more distant. Our present safety is built upon their risks, on their integrity, rebellion, and passion, and upon the courage that propelled them.

Part of the reckless hubris of our time is to believe that we have become so clever and complex as to render such qualities superfluous. We are assured that if we are competitive and hip enough, if we just obey the rules of the marketplace, all will be well.

Yet, as Lily Tomlin said, even if you win the rat race, you are still a rat. And there is another irony. The rules of the marketplace recreate the brutality, unfairness, and helplessness that humans have sought to escape for most of their evolution. Only during the last iota of our history have at least some finally broken away from tyrannies of nature and culture to build societies hospitable to the free individual. No small part of this work has occurred in our own land.

Rather than acting as stewards of this fragile achievement, we have lately become indifferent toward its lessons and profligate with its rewards. Too many, particularly in places of power, have become the spoiled brats of human progress.

For the rest, there is seldom power commensurate with available conscience or opportunities enough for available will. Worse, in the land of the bottom line, virtue not only fails to be its own reward, it is often undermined and becomes an object of ridicule.

To survive in such a time, to retain the will to be human, to build good communities, and to be decent and caring in such places, is extraordinarily difficult. The carelessly powerful are not about to tell us how. We must help each other.

What follows is my contribution to this common endeavor. It explores, among other things, the last great American taboo, namely struggle and failure — save that safely segregated as fiction or lyrics, or when we already know the happy ending.

In our own lives, however, we don't know the ending. To guide us along the way, a ubiquitous media beams relentless images of manic triumph alternating with failure's just deserts — arrest, death, defeat, and derision. There is little time for the lives of quiet desperation that Thoreau thought most of us led.

The advocate, the committed, the seeker, the free thinker, and the rebel thus may live in a world that is seldom depicted, let alone honored. They may be ignored, disparaged, or even punished; they may lack constituency, funds, or moral support. They may, like the urban itinerant Joe Gould, feel most at home "down among the cranks and misfits and the one-lungers and might-have-beens and the would-bes and the never-wills and the God-knows-whats." Yet, in the end, they can still attain that most precious victory of remaining truly human.

This book is written for the long courageous and for the newly restless. The first four chapters discuss our present condition in an effort to examine honestly our losses, frustrations, and dangers, not as abstract matters of state and society but as they affect each one of us. The second six chapters attempt to help the reader through a maze of faulty promises and failed prophets in order to consider some of the possibilities that remain — informed by history, philosophy, religion, anthropology and the tales of those who remind us we do not make this journey alone.

Life is a endless pick-up game between hope and despair, understanding and doubt, crisis and resolution. "Ever more," Emerson said of it, "is this marvelous balance of beauty and disgust, magnificence and rats." Sisyphus nears the mountaintop and the rock rolls down again. We lose courage and suddenly there is a light. What follows reflects this contest in which the grim and the glad are only oscillations and never the end.

For such reasons, I'll speak of possibilities and not of solutions, for it is in the abundance of our choices rather than in the perfection of our path that our future lies. And I'll not dwell on hope and faith because, central as they may be to our lives, far too many politicians, preachers, and publishers have used such words to defer present responsibilities, opportunity, and consciousness. It has been wisely said that "hope don't pay the cable" and faith is too often just another drug, producing hallucinogenic visions of a flawless future. This is not to reject either but rather to return them to their rightful role, that of planting seeds of possibility instead of sowing false prospects.

Are these possibilities enough? Well, they have served others in far more dismal times. We have come to expect more — including the entitlement of certitude. Hence, we sometimes approach these concerns much as though we were apostles out on a Saturday shopping for a creed. If this is you, I'm afraid I can't help you. You've come to the wrong door. There's nobody here but another member of the search party. Let's step into the sunlight together and see what we find.

PROBLEMS

Losses

Targets

False Profits

Despair and Survival

LOSSES

Over lunch one day, I asked journalist Stephen Goode how he would describe our era. Without hesitation, he said it was a time of epigons.

An epigon, he explained to my perplexed frown, is one who is a poor imitation of those who have preceded. The word comes from the *epigoni* — the afterborn — specifically the sons of the seven Greek chieftains killed in their attempt to take Thebes. The kids avenged the deaths by capturing Thebes — but they also destroyed it. They were generally not considered as admirable and competent as their fathers.

Being around epigons is like being trapped at a bad craft fair where everything you see seems to have been made before, only better. A *New York Times* article captured our epigonic era in full flower. The paper quoted the head of a TV production studio:

> We go into development meetings after they see how all their shows are failing, and they tell us we have to give them our wildest, most creative ideas.
>
> So we tell our writers to come up with the most original ideas they can. Then we come back and we've got about eight ideas to pitch, four that are truly out there and four that are more like original spins on familiar formats.
>
> The first thing that happens is they throw out the four wilder ideas because they're just too risky. Then they start to tinker with the others. And every change they suggest makes the show more conventional. Then they give us a list of actors and say don't cast anyone not on this list. Then there's a list for directors. And by the time they get the shows, they wonder why they have no original ideas.

In anthropology class I was first introduced to the notion, revolutionary for its time, that progress was not inevitable, that there can be an ebb as well as a flow to cultures. In one American archeology course we studied the steadily improving design of a tribe's pottery. As time passed, the browns and the blacks and the whites and the zigs and the zags became ever more intricate and appealing. But then cultural entropy set in and it all started to go the other way, the art a poor imitation of its predecessors. In short, the tribe forgot what it once had known.

Like the tribe, we have also forgotten much about ourselves. To be sure, this is not something we talk about, but to older Americans there is no point to the pretense. They remember the victories and their celebrations; they remember Norman Rockwell men standing motionless for the national anthem in baseball stadiums with fedoras held over their hearts; a government that did more than regulate or arrest you; politicians who were revered; newscasters who were trusted; the cop you met by name rather than with suspicion; and music that dripped syrup over our spirits and made them sweet and sticky. They remember when there was a right and wrong and who and what belonged with each, whether it was true or not. They remember a time when those in power lied and were actually able to fool us. They remember what a real myth was like even when it was false, cruel, deceptive, and the property of only a few.

Now, despite the improved economic and social status of women and minorities, despite decades of economic progress, despite Velcro, SUVs, MTV, NASA, DVDs, cell phones, and the Internet, you can't raise a majority that is proud of this country. We neither enjoy our myths nor our reality. We hate our politicians, ignore our moral voices, and distrust our media. We have destroyed natural habitats, created the nation's first downwardly mobile generation, stagnated their parent's income, and removed the jobs of each to distant lands. We have created rapacious oligopolies of defense and medicine, and frittered away public revenues. Our leaders and the media speak less and less of freedom, democracy, justice, or of their own land. Perhaps most telling, we are no longer able to react, but only to gawk.

To be sure, many of the symbols of America remain, but they have become crude — desperately or only commercially imitative of something that has faded. We still stand for the *Star Spangled Banner* but we no longer know what to do while on our feet. We still subscribe to the morning paper but it reads like stale beer. And some of us still even vote but expect ever less in return. Where once we failed to practice our principles, now we no longer even profess to honor them.

An awfulness is drifting over us. Too many have become obsessed with what we should ignore and ignore what we should celebrate or fear. Too many have lost the capacity for either grace or decency, preferring instead tricks and treachery.

A culture that has so lost its way and forgotten so much is not the same as a flawed society bumbling through history trying to make itself better. A civil rights veteran compared his era with the end of the century by saying that in the 1960s there had been hope that someday the Congress, the courts, and the White House would see the right. Now, he said, we no longer have that hope.

Worst of all, society lays the burden of its own failure upon each of us. Just as a strong culture buoys the individual and provides a stage upon which the brave, the compassionate, and the imaginative can act, so a craven, crumbling culture makes every act of individual will that much harder. Let's look at a few of the ways.

Reality

Sometime around the middle of the 1980s I suddenly noticed that the truth was no longer setting people free; it was only making them drowsy. This realization first came in the midst of a meeting held to discuss a worthy investigative journalism project. We had considered every aspect of the proposal save one and now, unbidden, a heretical question wiggled into my mind, never to leave: did the truth being sought really matter anymore?

At first it was only a sense of unease, a recognition that saying something true no longer commanded the respect it once had, an awareness that journalism was being driven away from the real and towards imaginings, mythologies, and "perceptions," that news itself was disappearing from the evening news and from newspapers, its place taken by inflated and clichéd descriptions, commentaries, and analyses of the news for which there was no longer any room.

We were, I had belatedly noticed, embarked upon an age that denied the existence of objective truth and, by extension, the value of any facts that might point to it. This was now an age, as philosophy professor Rick Roderick put it, when everything once directly lived was being turned into a representation of itself — news no less than anything else. As one frustrated television journalist explained, "I used to be a reporter for the *Washington Post*; now I play one on TV."

In the end we are left not with reality but with a recreated memory of reality, the repeated replacement of human experience. We watched Michael Jordan, Roderick argued, to remember what a life filled with physical exertion was about. Similarly, it can be said that we view C-SPAN to remember what democracy was about, just as we watched the Yugoslavian conflict on CNN for a sanitized recollection of war.

But if there is no value in truth and the real, then there is no value in pursuing any lack of these qualities. If nothing is real then what is left to report other than the image of what was once real? Hence the disappearance of facts from the media and their replacement by polls, pronouncements, and perceptions. Hence the growing feeling as we catch the evening news that we are watching a movie about television news that we've already seen and didn't like much.

Even more troubling questions emerge. If there is no reality, what guides us in our choices? Do we simply become one more perception that we market to other perceptions?

Everywhere we turn we are confronted with the hegemony of the artificial, the sovereignty of the fake. Of course, for the tourist, the television viewer, or the consumer, this is nothing new. In 1975 Umberto Eco wrote an essay, *Travels in Hyperreality*, in which he provided a field guide to some of America's many counterfeit cultural destinations. He described, for example, the reproduction of the 1906 drawing room of Mr. and Mrs. Harkness Flagler in the Museum of the City of New York, a drawing room that was itself inspired by the *Sala dello*

Zodiaco in the Ducal Palace of Mantua. The museum thus was offering its visitors a reproduction of a reproduction. Eco also tells of going, within 24 hours, from the fake New Orleans of Disneyland to the real city where a paddle-wheeler captain said it was possible to see alligators on the banks of the river but in fact was unable to produce any and "you risk feeling homesick for Disneyland, where the wild animals don't have to be coaxed. Disneyland tells us that technology can give us more reality than nature can."

One of Disney's later projects was the recreation of the Catholic Church in a TV series about a priest. The question of whether Disney's image was faithful to the church became not only a matter of considerable controversy but "news." Could Disney do for God what it had done for alligators? Hail Minnie full of grace?

One of those mediating this pseudo-crisis as a member of the Disney board was a (real) man of the cloth who also ran Georgetown University. At one point he found himself helping a group of Hollywood moguls decide whether a fake priest should be considered an actual heretic. He eventually joined the moguls in granting absolution, but how could even a good Jesuit be sure any more?

It's no longer just about show business. The synthetic images once largely contained within the spheres of entertainment, recreation and culture have become ubiquitous. It is no accident that Disney subsequently turned to remaking that most brutally honest of America's landscapes, the urban downtown. We all live in the theme park now.

In fact, an extraordinary portion of the gross domestic product is currently devoted to deception in one form or another, concealed though it may be as marketing, advertising, management, leadership seminars, news, entertainment, politics, public relations, religion, psychic hotlines, education, ab machine infomercials, and the law.

We have become a nation of hustlers and charlatans, increasingly choosing attitude over action and presentation over performance and becoming unable to tell the difference. It's not all that surprising because, whether for pleasure, profit, or promotion, and in ways subtle and direct, our society encourages and rewards those who out-sell, out-argue, and out-maneuver those around them — with decreasing concern for any harm caused along the way. As they say in Hollywood, the most important thing is sincerity. Once you've learned how to fake that, the rest is easy.

Anything in the culture that remains true to itself becomes a target. You want to emulate the 1950s and sit out your alienation in a coffee house? Sorry, you're too late. Starbucks, Brothers and Xando have the franchise.

You want to retreat to the world of ideas, to reflection on the choices that remain? To insist on freedom? To recover choice? Well, you won't be alone. Just turn on your TV:

Gentlemen, I'm going to read you your rights. You have the right to be strong, to be healthy, to strive, the right to make your own choices . . . And when it comes to your hair you have the right to choose Pantene Pro-V.

Or:

Freedom . . . to choose the best-tasting cola. That's what Royal Crown has stood for ever since it was first created in Columbus, Georgia, back in 1905. The freedom to decide who you are and what you drink. There's nothing more American than that. So, be free. Drink RC.

Or:

Soft drinks bring people together and provide the quilt of American diversity with a common ground on which to meet, enjoy and agree. By any measure, soft drinks are one of the important elements that bind American enterprise and culture into a system envied the world over.

What is going on here is the conversion of concepts central to our history, our politics, and our philosophy into mere merchandise. Capitalist personal trainer Tom Peters wants the young and ambitious to do the same with themselves: "Starting today, you're every bit as much a brand as Nike, Coke, Pepsi or the Body Shop."

James Atlas, writing in the *New Yorker* on the Harvard Business School, describes a classroom video in which Ogilvy & Mather CEO Charlotte Beers tells her advertising agency employees what went wrong with that classic marketing failure, "New Coke." People rejected the product, Beers said, "because the brand is owned by the people who consume it . . . I had my first kiss while I had a bottle of Coke in my hand . . . Coke isn't about taste; it's about my life."

Asked to explain why Campbell's Soup was such a powerful brand, one of the Harvard students replied, "I was thinking about my life in general and Campbell's Soup came to mind. I know it sounds crazy, but I thought a lot about the sustainability of it as a brand. When I was a little kid, you know, you always think, mmm, good."

Of course, owning or becoming a brand can be time-consuming. While a philosophy or religion can hold sway for centuries, the collapse of a product-based identity — whether it be that of a cool dude or a cool soda — can occur swiftly. Being someone was hard enough when it was just a matter of faith; now one is constantly in danger of falling into that huge, painful purgatory between the avant garde and retro.

As I walk along Washington's streets of power, I try to guess what all the suave and important-looking people around me actually do for a living. Is the brush-cut, with the shades the width of a tongue depressor, a stock clerk or a law student? Is the hyped-heel, cell-phoner brushing impatiently by me badly needed on Capitol Hill or is she, perhaps, the woman who will ring up my books later that day at Kramer Books?

We live in a time of democratic disguises when everyone — at least until they reach their place of employment — can be whoever they want. A nation of poseurs treating life as though it were an endless masque ball. Those who fail at the deception are the poor, the fat, the shy, the awkward, and the otherwise terminally déclassé. For the rest, a manic preoccupation with style and attitude tempts them to become not a reflection of who they are but who they want others to think they are.

Our primary business as Americans is to fool each other. Our tools come not from religion or politics but from the modern corporation. Hence the quiz shows that reward those who have absorbed most precisely the marketing messages transmitted to them. Hence the modern writing genre in which brand names replace generic adjectives. Our angst has become not that of the existentialist but of the discriminating shopper, witness the *New York Times* writer who summed up his 23-paragraph crisis as, "can a white consumer really get away with wearing a product designed and marketed by a youthful African-American company whose very name is a rallying cry of racial solidarity and economic empowerment?"

Juliette Guilbert in the weekly, *Generation Next*, was no less challenged as she examined the consumptive effluvia of 1950s retro. What does it mean, she somberly asked, that so many young people are "fetishizing a period before rock and roll, before women's liberation, before Civil Rights?"

As I wander down the aisles of these verbal WalMarts, I likewise feel a terrible burden for, as Guilbert put it, "like it or not, everyone who buys a vintage toaster is engaged in a culturally significant activity." If this is true, then who has time for politics or ideas?

Even sex, which is what people did for virtual reality before computers and White House communications directors came along, has been affected. For example, a *San Francisco Chronicle* story described a form of unprotected gay group sex that takes place with the knowledge that one participant is HIV-positive. This practice had earned criticism, especially from gay activists working to protect their kind from disease. Tom Coates, the director of an AIDS research institute panned an aggressively non-judgmental gay magazine article by Michael Scarce for not only "sensationalizing the movement but for not presenting a balanced view. Nowhere did I see the word 'responsibility.' As an HIV-infected man myself, I take that responsibility very seriously."

The *Chronicle* then continued:

Mr. Scarce dismisses the highly respected AIDS expert as part
of an "old guard" whose vision of HIV prevention is grounded
in the experience of baby boomers devastated by the epidemic.
. . . To younger homosexual men such as Mr. Scarce, AIDS has
become interwoven as part of homosexual identity. "AIDS and
gay culture are permanently tethered to one another, and not
necessarily in a bad way," he says.

Note that Coates' offense was not one of fact or even of motive, but rather of
age, attitude, and image. Who needs the National Institute of Health when a
hipper perspective will do the job just as well?

◆ ◆ ◆

The problem with having one's culture defined in such a manner is that the
once persistent and predictable tyranny of elders, church, and chieftains
becomes one controlled by a fickle and ever-changing semiotic oligopoly guided
primarily by what it thinks you want. These shamans of symbolism project back
on us a kind of virtual individualism, telling us how we should behave if we
were as free as they make us look in their ads. In return, we wear their logos to
say, yes, that's really is the sort of person we think we are. Or would like to be.

In a society informed by theme park information and run by theme park
rules, replacement reality becomes the property of the management. Life
becomes a giant magic show in which the audience is not allowed to see the real
action or the mechanisms that create the real action, but only a dramatization
of the action. Our participation is limited to the consumption of false images
and false words as we become permanent hostages of the prestidigitators.

Even a moderately skeptical and energetic media might help us remember
again. But the media is an essential part of the legerdemain, making information ever more a lever of control rather than of freedom. Just to glimpse the
problem could change the way a journalist wrote or spoke of the world. But the
rules of the magic kingdom rigidly discourage that. In a postmodern world,
truth is part of the privilege of power and to question received truth is to forego
received power. As Michael Parenti put it, reality itself has become radical. To
speak on its behalf is a form of insurrection.

Writer David Edwards, in an interview in the literary journal, *The Sun*, put
it this way:

I often feel a strange internal conflict between what I know is
true — what every cell in my body tells me is true — and what
I am told is true in the media and elsewhere. It's almost as if we
hypnotize ourselves into believing these absurdities. The key, I

suspect, is that everyone around us appears to accept what might otherwise be considered absurd. Then that small, lonely insecure part of us that likes to belong, that is terrified of being alone, thinks, *Well, that must be right* — not out of reason, but out of fear of isolation . . .

◆ ◆ ◆

The destruction of reality was already old hat to Umberto Eco by the mid-'60s. In 1967 he was writing of remedies. In *Towards a Semiological Guerrilla Warfare* he noted that "Not long ago, if you wanted to seize political power in a country, you had merely to control the army and the police . . . Today a country belongs to the person who controls communications."

To the conventional mind, a proper response to such a phenomenon would be to wrest control from those in power. Eco thought this might produce only skimpy results and offered an alternative:

> The battle for the survival of man as a responsible being in the Communications Era is not to be won where the communications originates, but where it arrives . . . A political party that knows how to set up a grass-roots action that will reach all the groups that follow TV and can bring them to discuss the message they receive can change the meaning that the source had attributed to the message. An educational organization that succeeds in making a given audience discuss the message it is receiving could reverse the meaning of that message. Or else show that the message can be interpreted in different ways.

Such a reordering of the news on arrival, rather than during creation, has been traditional in minority communities where understanding reality remains closely related to survival. But perhaps the most dramatic and revolutionary example of rearranging information is to be found on the Internet, which is one of the last media ecologies still hospitable to truth.

The Net allows anyone with a little technology to deconstruct the news in any manner and be assured of at least some audience. To be sure, the quality varies from the brilliant to the wrong to the absurd, but that is a small price to pay for relief from the mediocre, monochromatic, and manipulative alternative. To replace Big Brother with an infinite number of little siblings. To have choice again.

The mediacrats and the government sense the danger and have launched a fierce war for control. This, and not sex or national security, is what the debate over the Internet is really about. A few signs:

- Cokie and Steve Roberts wrote a column, headed INTERNET COULD BECOME A THREAT TO REPRESENTATIVE GOVERNMENT, warning against the direct democracy of the Internet and saying it could threaten the "very existence" of Congress.
- A commentator on *Court TV* argued that acceptance of government regulation of the Net was the equivalent of growing up.
- Leslie Stahl on *60 Minutes* called for the removal of undesirable information from the Net. Asked on what grounds, Stahl replied, "That it's wrong, that it's inaccurate, it's irresponsible, that it is spreading fear and suspicion of the government; 10,000 reasons."
- A writer in the *Washington Post* warned that without gatekeepers of information — e.g., the *Washington Post* — "our media could become even more infested with half-truths and falsehoods."
- *On Crossfire*, Geraldine Ferraro breathlessly warned that "we've got to get this Internet under control."
- A front page story in the *New York Times* was headlined TERM PAPERS ARE HOT ITEMS ON THE INTERNET. Other horrors in the *Times'* series included a story that the Net had caused Dartmouth students to forget sex, socializing and drinking; another on how to spot your computer addiction; and, finally, how the same technology that encourages celibacy at Dartmouth encourages flagrant and prolific sex everywhere else.

Those not in media elite have found something quite different on the Net. They are creating a cyberarchy of transformation — as different from the hierarchy of traditional information and politics as the vast wilderness of America was from the taut geography of 19th century Europe. The old dukes and baronets, clinging to their decadent landscape of conventional thought, rail against the primitiveness, the raucousness, the freedom of the new media, but theirs is effete whining in a happy hubbub of people discovering the ubiquitous potential of a new frontier with its fertile soil for the real. With the heady discovery of how many of us there really are has come a sense of incipient rebellion based not on ideology but on dreams and values — a shared faith that truth, freedom, the individual, community, and decency still matter.

Social democracy

It wasn't always like this. Grown politicians did not always go around ripping apart the normal functions of government just so they could claim to have balanced a budget. People who called themselves leaders did not pride themselves on setting citizen against citizen, or trying to see how many criminals they could fry, immigrants they could deny medical care and education, or welfare mothers they could further disparage. Reform was not always used by press and politicians as a euphemism for repeal.

From the start of the New Deal to the end of Jimmy Carter's tenure, the main course of American domestic politics was directed towards the improvement of life for the average citizen. The pace might vary markedly and the methods change, but not until the arrival of Ronald Reagan did power turn massively inward — determined to serve itself firstly and mostly.

Even that otherwise egregious warlock of Whittier, Richard Nixon, practiced domestic affairs in the tradition of social democracy. He was, in fact, our last liberal president, an amazing claim until one considers that he favored a negative income tax; revenue sharing; a guaranteed income for children; supplementary programs for the aged, blind, and disabled; uniform application of the food stamp program; better health insurance programs for low income families; aid to community colleges; aid to low-income college students; the creation of the National Endowment for the Humanities; and increased funding for elementary and secondary schools. Today someone of Nixon's domestic political tendencies might be considered too radical for C-SPAN.

With Reagan and subsequent presidents — again without respect to the party in the White House — politics drastically changed. In the place of social democracy came a bipartisan effort to repeal decades of American social and economic progress. Since then the moral burden has been shifted away from collective social responsibility towards increasing sanctions against transgressors and laggards, indifference towards the victims of moral apathy, and a government free to do whatever it wants.

Those too young to have remembered productive liberalism — before the species became a rigid, profligate, incompetent parody of itself — easily accepted the idea that our problems were due not to faults of those in currently in power but to the very policies that had helped create the comfortable perches from which the successful so loudly complained.

Such developments were complimented by efforts of major corporations to get Americans to accept a lower standard of living, albeit cleverly concealed in the rhetoric of economic growth. For the bulk of Americans not playing the stock market, the end of the century told a less than glorious story:

> ◆ Poor black families were working 190 hours more a year
> —— and poor white families 22 hours more — than in
> 1979 for roughly the same pay.

- While the income of middle-class, married-couple families grew 9% from 1989 to 1998 these families were working six extra full-time weeks a year to earn it.
- Over half of employees said that their company did not genuinely care about them.
- CEOs were earning 107 times that of the average worker, compared to 56 times in 1989.
- The top 1% of households in 1997 held 40% of the nation's wealth in 1997 compared to 25% in 1980. The combined wealth of the top 1% of US families was about the same as that of the entire bottom 95 percent.
- Ten percent of the U.S. population owned 82% percent of the real estate, 82% of the stock, and 72 % of the country's total wealth.
- Adjusted for inflation, the income of a recent male high school graduate declined 28% between 1973 and 1997.
- In 1939 a farmer had to produce 729 bushels of wheat to pay for his tractor. In 1999 a American farmer had to produce almost 23,000 bushels to pay for his new tractor.
- In 1997, almost half of the new jobs created paid less than $16,000
- The two richest men in America — Bill Gates and Warren Buffet — owned more assets than the bottom 45% of the country.

What corporate America wanted was nothing less than the Third Worlding of the US, a collapse of both present reality and future expectations. The closer the life and wages of our citizens could come to those of less developed nations, the happier the huge stateless multinationals would be. Then, as they said in the boardrooms and at the White House, the global playing field would be leveled.

Once having capitulated on economic matters, Americans would be taught to accept a similar diminution of social programs, civil liberties, democracy, and even some of the most basic governmental services. Free of being the agent of our collective will, government could then concentrate on the real business of a corporatist state, such as reinforcing the military, subsidizing selected industry, and strengthening police control over what would inevitably be an increasingly alienated and fractured electorate. We would be taught to deny ourselves progress and to blame others for our loss.

Worse, underneath the *sturm und drang* of political debate, the American establishment — from corporate executive to media to politician — reached a remarkable consensus that it no longer had to play by any rules but its own. There is a phrase for this in some Latin American countries: the culture of impunity. In such places it has led to death squads, to the live bodies of dissidents being thrown out of military helicopters, to routine false imprisonment and baroque financial fraud. We are not there yet but are certainly moving in the same direction.

In a culture of impunity, rules serve the internal logic of the system rather than whatever values typically guide a country, such as those of its constitution, church or tradition. The culture of impunity encourages coups and cruelty, at best practices only titular democracy, and puts itself at the service of what Hong Kong, borrowing from fascist Germany and Italy, refers to as "functional constituencies," which is mainly to say major corporations.

A culture of impunity varies from ordinary political corruption in that the latter represents deviance from the culture while the former becomes the culture. Such a culture does not announce itself. It creeps up day by day, deal by deal, euphemism by euphemism. The intellectual achievement, technocratic pyrotechnics, and calm rationality that serves as a patina for the culture of impunity can be dangerously misleading.

In a culture of impunity, what replaces constitution, precedent, values, tradition, fairness, consensus, debate and all that sort of arcane stuff? Mainly greed and power. As Michael Douglas put it in *Wall Street*: "Greed, for lack of a better word, is good. Greed is right. Greed works." Of course, there has always been an overabundance of greed in America's political and economic system. But a number of things have changed. As activist attorney George LaRoche points out, "Once, I think, we knew our greedy were greedy but they were obligated to justify their greed by reference to some of the other values in which all of us could participate. Thus, maybe 'old Joe' was a crook but he was also a 'pillar of the business community' or 'a member of the Lodge' or a 'good husband' and these things mattered. Now the pretense of justification is gone and greed is its own justification."

The result is a stunning lack of restraint. We find ourselves without heroism, without debate over right and wrong, with little but an endless narcissistic struggle by the powerful to get more money, more power, and more press than the next person. In the chase, anything goes and the only standard is whether you win, lose, or get caught.

◆ ◆ ◆

The major political struggle has become not between conservative and liberal but between ourselves and our political, economic, social and media elites. Between the toxic and the natural, the corporate and the communal, the technocratic and the human, the competitive and the cooperative, the efficient and the just, meaningless data and meaningful understanding, the destructive and the decent.

If you look around the country, though, you can see the outlines of a new political and cultural fault line — so new that it lacks a name, stereotypes, clichés, experts and prophets. In many ways it seems more a refugee camp than a voluntary assembly. On one side are libertarians, ethnic minorities, greens, populists, some unions, free thinkers, the alienated apathetic, the rural abandoned, the apolitical young, as well as others convinced that America is losing its democracy, its ground rules, and its soul. On the other side is the technological, media, legal, business and cultural elite of both major parties, centered in New York, Los Angeles, San Francisco, and Washington. At times it feels as if all of America outside of these centers has turned into a gigantic, chaotic *salon des refusés*. It is in this great room, no matter how strange and variegated, that a new future will have to be formed.

Time and space

Urban sociologist Claude S. Fisher writes that "our species has lived in permanent settlements of any kind for only the last two percent of its history." As late as the 1850s, just two percent of the world's population lived in cities of more than 100,000, by 1900 only about 10 percent. At the end of the last century, however, about half the world's humans lived in cities. In America, fewer than a quarter of us occupy a physical environment that is not primarily manufactured — a place in which time and space are not mainly defined by nature rather than by other human beings.

In fact, there are now more people in prison in than there are farmers, which is to say that you are more likely to find an American being kept in a cage than you are to find one who is raising corn or cattle. In two centuries America has moved from frontier to supermax.

My first diurnal sign of temporal and spatial control often comes with the morning news — "police activity," the local public radio station strangely calls it, a euphemism which could mean a burning tractor-trailer, a multi-car crash, or the diaspora of construction, but certainly means a delay for those who happen to be in the wrong place at the wrong time.

Washington's Capital Beltway hosts many of these incidents. It was completed in 1968. Since then the population of the metropolitan area has doubled. Meanwhile, on the West Coast, according to planners at Berkeley, San Franciscans are losing about 90,000 hours a day sitting in traffic jams. That's the amount of hours considered normal.

All around us are rules, exigencies, interruptions, and delays caused by ever more of us wanting to do the same thing at the same time. The line at the movie or nightclub. The restaurant with no table until 9:30; the hotel that is booked; the sign on the Massachusetts Pike warning that rest rooms at the next service area are limited.

The cause of these delays is a world in which nearly 11,000 people are added every hour, creating a new population the size of Newark, NJ each day. If nothing changes, America will be double what we are now by about 2058.

Which means, as former Gaylord Nelson has pointed out, twice as many cars, trucks, planes, airports, parking lots, streets, bridges, tunnels, freeways, houses, apartment buildings, grade schools, high schools, colleges, trade schools, hospitals, nursing homes, and prisons. Twice as much water and food if you can find it. Twice as many chemicals and other pollutants in the air and water, twice as much heat radiation from all the new construction, twice as much crime, twice as many fires, twice as big traffic jams, and twice as many walls with graffiti on them.

◆ ◆ ◆

Whenever I hear of another school shooting or other youthful violence, the first thing I think about is Dr. Calhoun and his mice. Dr. John Calhoun put four pairs of white mice in a steel cage eight-and-a-half feet on a side. Within two years the mice had increased to 2,200. The adult mice began excluding young mice from their company and the young began biting, attacking, and slashing one another. Finally social and sexual intercourse became impossible without violence. The mice stopped reproducing and eventually all died out.

We're in a cage, too, except it has shopping malls and freeways and cops with guns and sirens. We have governments and hospitals and schools and we have talk shows and newspapers to help us forget that we're in a cage.

But spend an evening surfing the channels and count the humans being destroyed — by crime, for fun, in sport. You can say it's television's fault, but, in the end, the producers and the reality cops and the extreme fighters are also in a cage, just like the viewers. Each is trying to control an environment over which they have lost control, whether using a gun, a ball, a camera, or a zapper. And it always ends in another confrontation: another ratings war, another arrest, another illegal deal, another TV pilot, another channel.

If you step back, there is madness in this, but if you think only of those in the cage — what they can hear, see, and understand — then a primal logic emerges, the need to restrain, suppress, or eliminate the proximate usurpers of one's rightful time and space. We don't talk about it much except when somebody suggests we might do it differently and then we say they are "thinking outside the box." Thinking and living inside a box is now more normal.

As with Dr. Calhoun's mice, the problem begins to reveal itself with the young. After World War II, spurred by a series of reports from Harvard president James Conant, America deliberately dismantled the education system that had brought it that far. Among other things, Conant considered the elimination of the small high school essential for the US to compete with the Soviets. America listened and between 1950 and 1970 the number of school districts in the country declined from 83,700 to 18,000. Schools increased in size, administration became centralized, principals became corporate executives and wardens rather than educators, and teachers became bureaucrats rather than prophets with honor in their own classrooms. And now we are giving up education itself in favor of cram courses. And now, again as a matter of premeditated national policy, we are reducing knowledge, wisdom, and survival to a matter of checking the right box. Standardized tests for standardized humans — without time or space for anything else.

◆ ◆ ◆

The corporations are doing their part. When I first read that we were being exposed to more than 3,000 advertising messages a day, I didn't believe it. Then I counted them as I walked the five blocks from my dentist to my office. Several hundred. Then I sat a suburban intersection and counted 50 before the light had turned green.

I think I don't pay attention to them but I do. At least some of the messages surrounding me push their way into my brain, shoving aside what was already there, perhaps only for a few seconds, perhaps never to be retrieved.

I don't protest because I have been taught that this is the way a city is meant to look. The fact that it didn't always look like this doesn't enter my thoughts because to me, as to everyone else, it doesn't seem that much worse than before. Which is to say, yesterday.

There are less obvious thieves of time and space. Such as the government. In the past 30 years the number of laws in our society has exploded, bearing little relationship to population growth, cultural complexity, or any other rational explanation. The number of lawyers have grown with it; in Washington there are nearly seven times as many attorneys as three decades ago. This is not the product of necessity. Neither is the explosion the product of ideology. Both liberals and conservatives have overstuffed the law shelves, albeit for different reasons.

But whatever the source, it now takes longer, requires more paper, and stirs up more intimations of liability to do almost anything worthwhile than it once did. While our rhetoric overflows with phrases like "entrepreneurship" and "risk-taking," the average enterprise of any magnitude is actually characterized by cringing caution with carefully constructed emergency exits leading from every corner of chance. We have been taught that were we to move unprotected into time and space, they might implode into us. Every law office is a testament to our fear and lack of trust.

Then there is the media, purportedly our surrogate priest, parent, and teacher, but in fact gangs of burglars breaking and entering our brains and stealing time and space. What was once extraordinary became merely unusual and finally universal as we moved from manuscript to microphone to camera and cable. With each step, context, environment, and points of reference became ever more distant and external. With each step, we became ever more dependent on things and people we would most likely never see in their unprojected, unfilmed, unrecorded nature. Sitting in a bar, riding an exercycle at the gym, or waiting in the airport, we trade proximate reality for a distant, visible, noisy but ultimately unreachable substitute. I even attended a wedding during which a large TV broadcast the NCAA championship in a room adjoining the reception hall. More than a few chose the ritual of the NBA over that of a traditional rite of passage. It just seems more natural to think inside the box. It is reality that has become strange.

♦ ♦ ♦

There is at present no politics of time and space, no reporters assigned to cover them, no time on their broadcasts nor space in their papers. And so we are confined in silence. We accept corporate trespassing on our hours and our acres with stunning passivity. We permit monitors in public areas to interrupt our conversation, distract our reading, and strain our conversation. Others spy on us. We turn much of what is left of our space and times over to our government, as though we considered ourselves no longer competent to handle it for ourselves.

There are, of course, exceptions. For example, the quarter of us who live in places of undefined range and unincorporated rhythms. Part of the political tension in America stems not so much from our differing ideologies as from our contrasting ecologies. It has been like that ever since the first adolescent left the farm for the city, but now the natural and the mechanical are too close to each other, symbolized by cell towers planted on our landscapes like great flagpoles of corporate conquerors.

Time and space were once an essential part of our nature. Gertrude Stein wrote that "in America there is more space where nobody is than where anybody is. This is what makes America what it is." By the 1950s, however, Alan Ginsberg was already speaking of "an America which no longer exists except in Greyhound bus terminals, except in small dusty towns seen from the window of a speeding car."

The deeply religious, the utopian, the cybernetic, and the fraternal can still escape into frontiers set at odd angles to the geographic. In fact, the freest people left in America may include the computer nerd and the contemplative nun, for each exist in a zone of tolerance for the human soul and imagination.

Others of us pass in and out, shaping our homes, our offices, our associations, and our families into temporary places of unregulated humanity, finding little oases in the desert of technocratic progress. Or we move furtively into the countryside, like Winston Smith escaping Big Brother, seeking what we have lost.

But most of it we do it either alone or in small, polite equivalents of the gangs to which urban adolescents gravitate in their search for something they haven't lost because they never had it. When we speak of time and space, we treat it as a personal problem. As if we were the only one too busy, too crowded, too behind the program projected on the schedule beaming up from our palm.

Typically, we passively accept the strip-mining of our time and space. We tolerate the grossest corporate graffiti while jailing the young who scrawl it just for love and attention instead of for market share. We let our children be huckstered in the classroom by Channel One when we could be destroying the magic of advertising by teaching them how it really works. We adapt to an explosion of prohibitions in our legal code, the invasion of our privacy to enforce them, and a government that is determined to scare us into doing precisely what it wants. And we remain far from that point described by ecologist Edward Abbey when we "draw a line across the ground of our home and our being, drive a spear into the land, and say to the bulldozers, earth movers, government and corporations, 'thus far and no farther.'"

The moral outsider

A common thread runs through our losses: the fading of the outsider of integrity, those to whom society has traditionally looked for moral guidance: teachers, ministers, writers, intellectuals, activists. What Weber called the pariah intelligentsia In short, those at the last ramparts of hope and faith, on the last battlement of the human spirit.

In Chaucer's time these people were called "clerks," which is to say someone other than a layman. For example, when we speak of a *cleric*, for example, we are hearkening back to when such a person would be known as a "clerk in holy orders." Today these "clerks" are known as academics, lawyers, writers and other members of the intelligentsia.

In the late 1920s, the French essayist Julien Benda wrote *La Trahison des Clercs*, which has been fairly translated as *The Treason of the Intellectuals*. Benda tells of Tolstoi seeing one of his brother Army officers strike a man who had fallen out of rank during a march. Tolstoi demanded: "Are you not ashamed to treat a fellow human being in this way? Have you not read the Gospels?"

The officer replied: "And have you not read Army Orders?"

Benda targeted "most of the influential moralists of the past 50 years in Europe" who had called "upon mankind to sneer at the Gospel and to read Army Orders." In other words, to replace morality with law and bureaucracy:

> At the end of the nineteenth century a fundamental change
> occurred: the clerks began to play the game of political passions.
> The men who had acted as a check on the realism of the people
> began to act as its stimulators.

We have seen the type in our time: the professors promoting the Vietnam War, the Henry Kissingers simultaneously playing conqueror and egghead; the

Arthur Schlesingers hard at work preserving the myths of the New Frontier; the Council on Foreign Relations; the nearly one-third of top Clinton aides who went to Harvard, Yale, or Georgetown, helping to drive the country far to the right and away from social and economic justice; the "conservative intellectuals" in the Bush administration spinning as hard as any PR flack.

Benda had them in his sights:

> At the very top of the scale of moral values they place the possession of concrete advantages, of material power and the means by which they are procured; and they hold up to scorn the pursuit of truly spiritual advantages, of non-practical or disinterested values.

Benda noted that while Plato believed that morality decided politics and Machiavelli believed that politics was beyond morality, now it was believed that politics should determine morality.

The new intellectuals favored many of the same principles popular among today's leaders. Among them:

- The extolling of courage at the expense of other virtues. This places the warrior, the aggressor, the "killer litigator," and the reckless higher in society than the wise, the just, and the sensible.
- "The extolling of harshness and the scorn for human love — pity, charity, benevolence."
- A cult of success . . . "the teaching which says that when a will is successful that fact alone gives it a moral value, whereas the will which fails is for that reason alone deserving of contempt."

In the 1920s, Benda foresaw a "future war when a nation would decide not to look after the enemy wounded," a society that prided itself for its freedom from "stupid humanitarianism," and even the coming of genocide: "The logical end of the 'integral realism' professed by humanity today is the organized slaughter of nations or classes."

Further, Benda saw the potential for a perverse form of reconciliation, driven by an understanding that the "thing to possess would be the whole earth," an "imperialism of the species preached by all the great directors of the modern conscience."

> In this way inter-human wars will come to an end. In this way humanity would attain 'universal fraternity.' But far from being the abolition of the national spirit with its appetites and its

arrogance, this would simply be its supreme form, the nation being called Man and the enemy God. Thereafter, humanity would be unified in one immense army, one immense factory, would be aware only of heroisms, disciplines, inventions, would denounce all free and disinterested activity, would long cease to situate the good outside the real world, would have no God but itself and its desires . . ."

In short, a globalized world that daily seems more familiar as we dispense with the need for any indices save those measuring the expansion of power and wealth. The new world order.

This order emanates from a mandarin class that is neither left or right. Its members often are the sort of which it has been said that when they are alone in a room, there is no one there. In such a culture the marketplace of ideas essentially shuts down. There is no longer any real politics, only deals. No victories, only leveraged buyouts. No ideology; only brand loyalty. No conservative and liberal, only Coke and Pepsi.

Remember: we are talking here of culture, not of conspiracies. If you have a strong enough culture you don't need a conspiracy. One of the reasons ethnic minorities and women continue to have such a hard time moving ahead is precisely because there is no one to blame, no smoking gun, nothing on paper — only an invisible wall of implicit values and ingrained behavior.

The mandarin class prides itself on its wisdom and intelligence, but its greatest true skill is the circumnavigation of guilt. No embarrassment is too great, no crisis too unnecessary, no expense too inexplicable, and no war too unjustified.

A language of exculpation develops. The candidacy of a woman running for the House of Representatives, already a bit rocky owing to her having killed somebody in 1979 in a case ruled self-defense, came to an end after she first denied, and then admitted, having also assaulted a state trooper 11 years earlier. Her withdrawal statement proved, however, that she was fully qualified to live in Washington: "Various stories appearing recently have made me realize that it will be difficult, if not impossible, to focus and discuss the meaningful issues of the campaign."

Among the powerful, "mistakes were made" but no one has to admit that they were the ones who made them. Instead, the elite rises as one to pronounce it not the time for blame, but rather for moving forward together into the future and putting this or that "behind us." Everyone nods their heads and the foxes are allowed back into the chicken house one more time.

All this is carried out with a numbing smugness. The prototypical member of the elite possesses, as Cromwell says in *A Man for All Seasons*, "a self-conceit that can cradle gross crimes in the name of effective action." Among the elite there is not even any particular loyalty to this country. More and more, its business is elsewhere; and it is shamelessly willing to use political power to further that business. It seeks greatly weakened countries in which stateless corporations and their managers are accountable to no one. Their only pledge of allegiance is to a trade agreement.

Like a hit and run driver, America's elite has left the scene of the accident. More and more, those who run this country have the character of wealthy, isolated strangers — armed but afraid, intrusive yet indifferent, personally profligate but politically penurious, priggish in rhetoric yet corrupt in action. No longer does national myth connect them with the greater mass of America. Nor, any longer, does politics separate them from each other; Republicans and Democrats have become, rather than choices, degrees of the same dismal thing.

They have become like those of whom Fitzgerald wrote in *The Great Gatsby*:

> They were careless people — they smashed up things and crea-
> tures and then retreated into their money or their vast careless-
> ness or whatever it was that kept them together, and let other
> people clean up the mess they had made.

And through this all — the unreal, the undemocratic, the amoral, the crowded, and the uncritical — the American individual walks alone.

TARGETS

Imagine living with someone who lied to you every day, took too much and gave too little, manipulated opportunities, denied responsibility, ordered you about, declined to accept advice, and refused to recognize any explicit or implicit contract between the two of you.

Dismal as this sounds, it is not a bad description of the relationship between ourselves and larger institutions with which we must increasingly deal. John McKnight describes the alternative — what he calls authentic social forms — as possessing three basic dimensions: "They tend to be uncommodified, unmanaged, and uncurricularized."

What happens when this is not so? Instead of friends and relatives mourning with us we have bereavement counselors turning grief into a commodity. Instead of a community, we have managers creating a bureaucracy. Instead of practical teachers, we have technocrats building rigid rules of learning.

There is now hardly a part of our lives that we can not turn over to someone else in order for it to be properly managed and controlled. A poignant example was offered by Dirk Johnson in the *New York Times* when he described the trend towards Little League personal trainers. One parent was paying $70 an hour to get his son up to par. Said his mother: "We did it for his self-esteem."

The owner of a firm that supplies trainers told Johnson, "On Monday morning, we get frantic calls from parents. They'll say, 'It's an emergency — the boy struck out twice on Saturday — we need help right away.'"

Bernard Beck, a sociologist at Northwestern University, told Johnson that child raising had taken a more management-style approach, especially among parents who were well-educated and successful. In some ways, Beck said, children have come to be seen a bit like growth stocks. He summed it up this way:

> In an earlier generations, parents were younger, going at life without much of a plan, a little courageous and a little foolhardy, a kind of what-the-heck attitude. But many of today's parents are more serious. They put off having children for a career. And having had success in their careers, they use the same goal-oriented principles when it comes to raising their kids. They study what's needed for success. They look at the competition. It's all a very rational, very market-oriented approach.

Even the humanities have been put in harness for management, as at the Aspen Institute which once offered a course called "Can the Humanities Improve Management Effectiveness?" The primary objectives: "To improve management effectiveness, to develop more competent and socially acclimated managers, and to assist in the success process of managers to executives."

In such ways has the manager replaced the priest, the politician, the teacher, and the artist in turn-of-the-century America. Boosted by the insidious myth that "management skills" can substitute for knowledge of what one is managing, as well as obviating the need for social intelligence and moral vision, Americans have rushed to emulate the very archetype that is successfully dismantling and desiccating their culture.

How strange it would be to find a modern manager writing to his nephew words such as these:

> Though you cannot see, when you take one step, what will be the next, yet follow truth, justice and plain dealing, and never fear their leading you out of the labyrinth, in the easiest manner possible. The knot which you thought a Gordian one, will untie itself before you. Nothing is so mistaken as the supposition that a person can extricate himself from a difficulty by intrigue, by chicanery, by dissimulation, by trimming, by an untruth, by an injustice.

Denying his nephew the standard weapons of contemporary business and politics might seem a disservice, but the uncle didn't do all that poorly at management. After all, Thomas Jefferson helped to organize a whole country.

John Ralston Saul put it plainly in *Voltaire's Bastards*, "Management cannot solve problems. Nor can it stir creativity of any sort. It can only manage what it is given. If asked to do more, it will deform whatever is put into its hands."

Even within the literature of management one can find evidence. Richard Lester in *The Productive Edge* reported that only a third of 500 surveyed companies felt that their much-touted "total quality management" programs had a significant impact on their competitiveness.

And Saul gives a devastating example of the limits of management:

> The Holocaust was the result of a perfectly rational argument — given what reason had become — that was self-justifying and hermetically sealed. There is, therefore, nothing surprising about the fact that the meeting called to decide on "the final solution" was a gathering mainly of senior ministerial representatives. Technocrats. Nor is it surprising that [the] Wansee Conference lasted only an hour — one meeting among many for those present — and turned entirely on the modalities for

administering the solutions . . . The massacre was indeed 'managed,' even 'well managed.' It had the clean efficiency of a Harvard case study.

Marshall Rosenberg, who teaches non-violent communication, was struck in reading psychological interviews with Nazi war criminals not by their abnormality, but that they used a language denying choice: "should," "one must," "have to." For example, Adolph Eichmann was asked, "Was it difficult for you to send these tens of thousands of people their death?" Eichmann replied, "To tell you the truth, it was easy. Our language made it easy."

Asked to explain, Eichmann said, "My fellow officers and I coined our own name for our language. We called it *amtssprache* — 'office talk.'" In office talk "you deny responsibility for your actions. So if anybody says, 'Why did you do it?' you say, 'I had to.' 'Why did you have to?' 'Superiors' orders. Company policy. It's the law.'"

Yet for all the words we have devoted to the Holocaust, go into almost any bookstore and you'll find far more works on how to manage, manipulate and control others – and how to use "office talk" — than you will on how to practice the skills of a free citizen. Some of the most important lessons of the Holocaust are simply missed. Among these, as Richard Rubenstein has pointed out, is that it could only have been carried out by "an advanced political community with a highly trained, tightly disciplined police and civil service bureaucracy."

In *The Cunning of History*, Rubenstein also finds uncomfortable parallels between the Nazis and their opponents. For example, in 1944 a Hungarian Jewish emissary meets with Lord Moyne, the British High Commissioner in Egypt, and suggests that the Nazis might be willing to save one million Hungarian Jews in return for military supplies. Lord Moyne's reply: "What shall I do with those million Jews? Where shall I put them?" Writes Rubenstein:

> The British government was by no means averse to the 'final solution' as long as the Germans did most of the work.

For both countries, it had become a bureaucratic problem, one that Rubenstein suggests we understand "as the expression of some of the most profound tendencies of Western civilization in the 20th century."

These tendencies are not alien to America. General Curtis LeMay ran the air war against both Japan and North Korea, became head of the sacrosanct Strategic Air Command, and was one of the military heroes of his time. Here are just a few of his accomplishments as reported by Richard Rhodes in the *New Yorker*:

- ♦ The destruction of nearly 17 square miles of Tokyo with the loss of at least 100,000 civilian lives.

- The destruction of 62 other Japanese cities. Only Hiroshima and Nagasaki were spared — reserved for their own special horror. In sum, more than a million Japanese civilians were killed. LeMay himself would admit years later, "I suppose if I had lost the war, I would have been tried as a war criminal. Fortunately, we were on the winning side."
- The bombing of North Korean cities, dams, villages and rice paddies. Civilian deaths: more than two million.

In short, with the enthusiastic blessing of the American government, LeMay was directly responsible for the slaughter of about half as many civilians as died in the Holocaust. And LeMay had even grander schemes. His plan for defeating the Soviet Union included the obliteration of 70 Soviet cities in 30 days with 33 atomic bombs and the deaths of 2.7 million citizens.

One of the reasons we don't hear much about such things is because the political center limits both the topics and the range of the debate. For example, imagine turning on C-SPAN and hearing a high government official say of another:

> [He is] actuated by views, in my judgment, subversive of the principles of good government and dangerous to the union, peace and happiness of the country.

And another high official replies the next day:

> His system flowed from the principles adverse to liberty and was calculated to undermine and demolish the republic.

This sort of language would cause extreme anchor anxiety but, in fact, is found, in the first case, in a letter by Alexander Hamilton concerning James Madison and, in the second instance, in a letter from Thomas Jefferson concerning Hamilton. At the time the letters were written, Hamilton was Secretary of Treasury and Jefferson was Secretary of State, both serving at the pleasure of George Washington, to whom each penned his screed.

Today, outlets such as C-SPAN and PBS function as karaoke bars of political centrism. Far from encouraging the sort of vibrant debate our country needs, they apply a verbal tourniquet to democracy by limiting how one may speak about it. In fact, what shocks some about less restrictive talk radio is really just the sound of democracy happening.

It's not just the media, though, that keeps debate in check. How many school children are taught that, worldwide, wars in the past century killed over 100 million people? In World War I alone, the death toll was around ten million. Much of this, including the Holocaust, was driven by a culture of modernity that so changed the power of institutions over the individual that the latter would become what Erich Fromm called *homo mechanicus*, "attracted to all that is mechanical and inclined against all that is alive." Becoming, in fact, a part of the machinery — willing to kill or to die just to keep it running.

Thus, with Auschwitz–like efficiency, over 6,000 people perished every day during World War I for 1,500 days. Rubenstein recounts that on the first day of the Battle of the Somme, the British lost 60,000 men and half of the officers assigned to them. But the internal bureaucratic logic of the war did not falter at all; over the next six months, more than a million British, French and German soldiers would lose their lives. The total British advance: six miles. No one in that war was a person anymore. The seeds of the Holocaust can thus be found in the trenches of World War I. Individuals had became no better than the bullets that killed them, just part of the expendable arsenal of the state.

◆ ◆ ◆

Today almost every principle upon which this country was founded is being turned on its head. Instead of liberty we are being taught to prefer order, instead of democracy we are taught to be follow directions, instead of debate we are inundated with propaganda. Most profoundly, American citizens are no longer considered by their elites to be members or even worker drones of society, but rather as targets — targets of opportunity by corporations and of suspicion and control by government.

It is not surprising, therefore, that an increasing number have come to accept our culture's message that their choices are largely ones of association: what they join (a corporation, church or organization), their innate "identity" (ethnicity or sex), or that which they consume (wine, clothing, car).

These are the brands we display on our clothes and in our speech and, most importantly, that march through our minds. Increasingly, our lives are being run by logos rather than logos, symbols rather than reason. The alternative notion — that one's identity is created by the conscious choices one makes — seems odd and archaic. Few are telling people — certainly not the government, media, or corporate America — that they still have a latent, common power to shuck their symbolic uniforms, to become themselves, to change what is happening to them.

Contemporary America actively opposes choice. Choice is repressed by a government that increasingly interferes in its citizens' personal lives; choice is manipulated by advertising and public relations; choice is distorted by mass media and the politicians it creates; it is limited by the growing homogeneity of commercial and cultural life, it is ignored by schools that prefer teaching drivers education to analytical skills, and it is suppressed by a cornucopia of illegal and legal drugs that allow one to avoid the pain and hard work of decisions — seductive relief from what Sartre called the "vertigo of possibility."

We easily observe and deplore the absence of choice when we see it in its adolescent form — such as in the gang — but we are less perceptive when it happens to us, especially when it occurs incrementally and in a climate that permits the evocation of what we used to be to conceal what we are truly becoming.

One example of these trends is the increase in laws aimed at social control rather than traditional criminality. Juvenile curfews, the penalizing of parents for the misdeeds of their young, and the drug war are all examples of government acting not only to prevent dangerous deviance but to enforce its definition of normalcy. Aside from frequently violating the Constitution, these acts steal freedom from citizens and habituate them to still further encroachments.

Why this happened so dramatically in the last two decades of the 20th century is a matter of conjecture. Certainly external factors didn't justify it, even using the crudest logic. But then, perhaps that was part of the problem. At the end of the Cold War, a top Soviet official promised America one last horrible surprise: the loss of an enemy. It was as the Greek poet Constantine Cavafy had written early in the century:

> Night is here but the barbarians have not come.
> And some people arrived from the borders,
> and said that there are no longer any barbarians.
> And now what shall become of us without any barbarians?
> Those people were some kind of solution.

A decade after the Cold War, a Pentagon office sported a sign that read, WANTED: A GOOD ENEMY. In fact the military was still shopping for new enemies to buck up the welfare fathers of the defense industry. These enemies were initially vague enough that they were known by such abstractions as a *generic composite peer competitor, myriad formless threats,* and even, God forbid, *normal asymmetrical niche opponent.* The search was not entirely futile; in a few years the military was in the air against Yugoslavia.

But there was another target starting to turn up in the planners' mind: the US citizen. For the first time since the Civil War, American government officials began seriously considering the possibility of armed conflict in, and occupation of, their own country. There was a growing assumption that the interests of those with power and those without might diverge to the point of insurrection.

The major media steadfastly ignored the trend despite ample evidence lying about. For example, *Defense Week* reported that "Army Chief of Staff Gen. Dennis Reimer said the Army needs to focus more on homeland defense and welcomes a 'mission creep' into that area." According to the *Army Times,* Defense Secretary William Cohen warned in 1998, "Terrorism is escalating to the point that Americans soon may have to choose between civil liberties and more intrusive means of protection." One year later, unheralded in most of the media, Cohen established a new homeland military command. Wrote *USA Today*, "The military must 'deal with the threats we are most likely to face,' Cohen said, brushing aside concerns about federal troops operating at home. 'The American people should not be concerned about it. They should welcome it.'"

What neither Cohen nor the media told the public was that the number of international terrorist attacks had actually declined 59% in the previous decade and that the total American casualties from terrorism in 1998 had been 24, compared with over a thousand five years earlier.

Still, a 1996 article by military historian and strategist Martin van Creveld in the *Los Angeles Times* argued that

> As the 20th century draws to an end, it is time that military commanders and the policy makers to whom they report wake up to the new realities. In today's world the main threat to many states, including specifically the US, no longer comes from other countries. Either we make the necessary changes, or what is commonly known as the modern world will lose all sense of security and dwell in perpetual fear.

Perhaps most startling was an article in the Winter 1992 issue of *Parameters*, a quarterly published by the US Army College. The author was Lt. Col. Charles J. Dunlap Jr., a graduate of Villanova School of Law, the Armed Forces Staff College, and a distinguished graduate of the National War College. He had been named by the Judge Advocates Association as the USAF's outstanding career armed services attorney. In short, not your average paranoid conspiracy theorist.

Dunlap's article was called "The Origins of the American Military Coup of 2012." In it, he pretended to be writing to a fellow military colleague in 2012, explaining how the coup had occurred. He accurately described America's current state:

> America became exasperated with democracy. We were disillusioned with the apparent inability of elected government to solve the nation's dilemmas. We were looking for someone or something that could produce workable answers. The one institution of government in which the people retained faith was the military. Buoyed by the military's obvious competence in the First Gulf War, the public increasingly turned to it for solutions to the country's problems. Americans called for an acceleration of trends begun in the 1980s: tasking the military with a variety of new, non-traditional missions, and vastly escalating its commitment to formerly ancillary duties.

Dunlap quoted one of Washington's journalistic cherubs, James Fallows, who wrote in a 1991 article

> I am beginning to think that the only way the national govern-ment can do anything worthwhile is to invent a security threat and turn the job over to the military . . . The military, strangely, is the one government institution that has been assigned legiti-macy to act on its notion of the collective good.

Fallows was not alone within the Washington establishment. Stephen Rosenfeld of the *Washington Post* wrote a column praising an Army advocate of Dunlap's nightmare. Rosenfeld described US Army Major Ralph Peters this way:

> At home, use of the military appears inevitable to him — though not yet to an American consensus — "at least on our borders and in some urban environments" . . . He deplores our military's reluctance to join the war on drugs, which he attrib-utes to a fear of failure. He would dutifully prepare for the tra-ditionally 'military' missions, plus the new one of missile defense. But he would be ready to engage with drugs and crime, terrorism, peacekeeping, illegal immigration, disease control, resource protection, evacuation of endangered citizens . . .

What Dunlap described and Peters advocated was not a bold military stroke against the civilian government, but simply a coup by attrition. Wrote Dunlap:

> By the year 2000 the armed forces had penetrated many vital aspects of American society. More and more military officers sought the kind of autonomy in these civilian affairs that they would expect from their military superiors in the execution of traditional combat operations . . . They convinced themselves that they could more productively serve the nation in carrying out their new assignments if they accrued to themselves unfet-tered power to implement their programs.

Dunlop's timing was a bit off, but there is little doubt he had spotted a trend. Since the article appeared, the military has, for example, engaged in numerous mock urban invasions and assaults, often unannounced and sometimes scaring the wits out of citizens with low-flying helicopter sorties in the middle of the night. Even some of the participants have had a hard time adjusting to the idea of invading one's own country. Said a Marine colonel of a West Coast exercise that was garnering local opposition, "Normally, we go into a country that's in some fatal stage. We work with those who are with us, and shoot those who are not. The part that's missing here is that you can't shoot the Coastal Commission."

In such ways have we become targets — part of the potential enemy. The game plan of America's mandarins assumes a widening gap between the governed and the governing and between rich and poor, one that may have to be met by force of one sort or another. Those in power are prepared to do business with most favored nations abroad and to suppress the least favored citizens at home.

This is a policy without redemption. It is not only economically cruel and profoundly anti-democratic, it is deeply subversive and destructive of American ideals and culture, not to mention our constitution. Those who run the country, whether in government, business or media, seldom speak of this land anymore with feeling, affection or understanding. They too often carry forth their affairs unburdened by place, history or culture — without conscience, without country, and without any sense of the pain they have caused.

America is no longer a place to serve and to love. Because they have, in the name of global glories, cut themselves off from their own land, it is becoming for them increasingly a place of danger — a place of long, grim shadows, the sort of shadows that too often conceal a foe.

How far are we along this road? David Ross, a science fiction author, sat down with a George Orwell scholar and found that more than 100 of the 137 predictions or indicators used in the novel *1984* had come to pass, including sensitive omni-directional microphones, two-way television, restricted turnoff options, wide angle lens, personal databanks, prose-writing machines, tone-of-voice analyzers, remote detection of a human heartbeat, rapid destruction of documents, police patrol helicopters, think tanks to plan future wars, doomsday research, self-propelled bombs, more lethal nerve gases, and tailored genetic diseases.

Orwell was prescient in less specific ways as well. One of the characteristics of his inner party, the less than two percent that controlled the rest, was that there was no sexual or racial discrimination. He understood that ethnic eradication, while characteristic of nazism, was not required for fascism, a point that would be missed by later generations who assumed that if a gay or a black was running the show we must still be in democracy mode.

In fact, one of the characteristics of the modern propaganda state is the use of positive ethnic and sexual iconography to cover its tracks. Thus Richard Nixon was slurring Jews in Oval Office conversations even as he set a new record in their high-level appointments. W.J. Clinton was called our first black president by Toni Morrison even as the government was sending young black males to prison in unprecedented numbers. And German Greens joined a governing coalition for the first time only to find themselves being used as part of the moral justification for the bombing of Yugoslavia.

Journalist Sam Yette described the function of minorities in such situations:

- They provide credibility for otherwise invalid products
- They are neutralized by being taken away from potential radical roles
- They provide minority leadership that can take responsibility for anti-minority policies and decisions.

Orwell also had a clear understanding of how an elite could control the rest of the masses. He described the "proles" who made up the better part of the country and the least part of its power:

> Heavy physical work, the care of home and children, petty quarrels with neighbors, films, football, beer, and above all, gambling filled up the horizon of their minds. To keep them in control was not difficult. A few agents of the Thought Police moved always among them spreading false rumors and marking down and eliminating the few individuals were judged capable of becoming dangerous; but no attempt was made to indoctrinate them with the ideology of the Party . . . From the proletarians nothing is to be feared. Left to themselves, they will continue from generation to generation and from century to century, working, breeding, and dying, not only without any impulse to rebel, but without the power of grasping that the world could be other than it is. . . .

Orwell would not have been surprised that the *Washington Post* a few years ago published Nathan Gardels' arguments for the US becoming an authoritarian society like Singapore. Said Gardels,

> Perhaps it is time to consider the possibility that the Western attitude that has all but cast away the notion of appropriate social authority might be outmoded. After all, the key problem of Western civilization now is not the absence of tolerance, it is how to cope with so much freedom.

Gardels quoted a senior Singapore official as saying, "The top three to five percent of a society can handle this free-for-all, this clash of ideas. If you do this with the whole mass . . . you'll have a mess." To be sure, the *Post* did run a blistering countering article. Nonetheless, the articles in tandem left the feeling of having witnessed a thoughtful debate on the virtue of using torture or reviving segregation. Besides, that same year the *Post* ran an article suggesting that democracy was not appropriate for many small countries. The article argued, among other things, that "freeing markets and foreign trade can be more important than freeing ballot boxes." And the ultra-establishment *Atlantic Monthly* promoted an article by Robert Kaplan saying, "The global triumph of democracy was to be the glorious climax of the American Century. But democracy may not be the system that will best serve the world . . ."

Why would a hard-won democracy willingly drift in such a direction? One reason is that if one is going to tolerate a growing divide between rich and poor, between those with power and those without, it is necessary to deal with the anger and alienation that results. If the traditional democratic approach — making the system fairer — is ruled out, then some form of oppression is required.

Besides, while a democratic redistribution of wealth and power might leave the country as a whole better off economically, it would be hard to convince those throwing million-dollar weddings or buying $70,000 personal submarines out of the Hammacher-Schlemmer catalog that this is the case.

Here is some of what has already happened in America's gated economy:

- 13% of black men have lost their right to vote because of felony convictions — 31% in Alabama.
- The number of misdemeanor charges in New York City increased 85% during the 1990s.
- 40% of all post-Civil War federal criminal laws have been passed since 1970.
- By the end of the 1990s, nations whose combined prison population could fit inside just California penal institutions with space left over included France, Great Britain, Germany, Japan, Singapore, and the Netherlands.
- The incarceration rate has tripled since the 1970s.
- In 1999 there was a one in four chance that a black child born that year would end up in jail.

If your goal is the economic well-being of the inner party rather than the general welfare, a strong case can be made that most people will accept their exclusion with quiet despair. Thus you can cut their services and deny them aid and they will not revolt. For those few who show signs of trouble, you simply write laws that restrict their employment, take away their driver's license, or ensure them incarceration using whatever ruse, such as drug laws, that works.

We know who might cause trouble. They are black, Latino, and white males with a high school education or less. They are the only sizable socio-economic minority in the country without a movement, without advocacy organizations, without media support. If they act out, if they smoke pot, have the wrong papers or otherwise get into trouble, we simply throw them in jail.

For less disruptive members of the society, the goal is not that they feel pain but that they not feel restless. Writing before the rise of Hitler, Aldous Huxley in *Brave New World* understood this principle; the people of his world took daily drugs, had plenty of access to sex, and were absorbed in such pre-Nintendo activities as obstacle golf. There were "feelies," movies that allowed you to touch as well as hear and see; diseases had been abolished; and death had been made as pleasant as possible.

Some of traits of Huxley's world sound eerily familiar, such as genetic engineering, a stress on identity instead of individuality, psychological conditioning, the planned and controlled pursuit of happiness, the use of drugs as a cultural sedative, mindless consumption and the destruction of the family.

♦ ♦ ♦

One of the reasons we have such difficulty perceiving our current conditions is our aversion to a single word: *fascism.* While there is no hesitation by politicians to draw parallels with the Holocaust to justify whatever foreign adventure appeals to them, or for the media to make similar analogies at the scrawl of a swastika, we seem only able to understand — or even mention — the climax of fascism rather than its genesis.

So removed is the true nature of fascism from our consciousness that it has even become of a fashion statement, as the *New York Times*' Ruth La Ferla described in an stunningly offhand manner:

> The brute aesthetic of fascism — a blend of classical style and modern functionalism advanced by 20th-century totalitarian regimes — is widespread these days, having muscled its way from the worlds of architecture and fashion photography onto movie screens and runways . . . Fashion's flirtation with fascism has, to be sure, been stripped of its darker political content. Still, the ponderous style identified with tyranny retains an allure. "Fascism — I hate to say it, but it's sexy," said Ned Cramer, a senior editor at Architecture magazine. The style generally is attractive, he said. "It expresses the idea of taking and then relinquishing control" . . .
>
> The aggressive style of totalitarianism retains a power to seduce because it "comes from a lineage of darkness," said Yeohlee Teng, a New York fashion designer . . . Brutal granite and travertine structures, the dictator's pet mode of propaganda, "are all about power," Ms. Teng said, "and power is the greatest turn-on."

Italians, who invented the term, also called it the *estato corporativo*: the corporatist state. Orwell rightly described fascism as an extension of capitalism. It is an economy in which the government serves the interests of oligopolies, a state in which large corporations have the powers that in a democracy devolve to the citizens.

Today, it is no exaggeration to call our economy corporatist, defined by British scholars R.E. Pahl and J. T. Winkler as a system in which the government guides privately owned businesses towards order, unity, nationalism and success. "Let us not mince words," they said. "Corporatism is fascism with a human face."

The Nazis had their own word for it: *wehrwirtschaft*, semantically linking wehr (for defense, bulwark, weapon) with *wirtshaft* (for housekeeping, domestic economy, husbandry) to describe an economy based on the assumption of warfare. The concept was not new, however. William Shirer points out in *The Rise and Fall of the Third Reich* that 18th- and 19th-century Prussia devoted 70% of its revenue to the army and "that nation's whole economy was always regarded as primarily an instrument not of the people's welfare but of military policy."

In Hitler's Germany even the pogroms were part of national economic planning, seizing Jewish shops and companies and replacing Jewish workers with the Ayran unemployed. Hitler argued that "private enterprise cannot be maintained in a democracy," and denounced "the freedom to starve," in a country which had known as many as six million without jobs. Wrote Shirer, "In taking away that last freedom, Hitler assured himself of the support of the working class."

The link between business and fascism was clear to German corporatists. Auschwitz was not just a way to get rid of Jews, it was also a major source of cheap labor. As Richard Rubenstein points out, "I.G. Farben's decision to locate at Auschwitz was based upon the very same criteria by which contemporary multinational corporations relocate their plants in utter indifference to the social consequences of such moves." I.G. Farben invested over a billion dollars in today's money at Auschwitz and, thanks to the endless supply of labor, adopted a policy of deliberately working the Jewish slaves to death.

In such ways do economics and freedom become intertwined. Those who think it can't happen here should consider that four days before Mussolini became Premier he met with a group of industrialists and assured them that his aim "was to reestablish discipline within the factories and that no outlandish experiments. . . . would be carried out." In *Friendly Fascism*, Bertram Gross notes that Mussolini also won "the friendship, support or qualified approval" of the American ambassador, Cornelius Vanderbilt, Thomas Lamont, many newspapers and magazine publishers, the majority of business journals, and quite a sprinkling of liberals, including some associated with both *The Nation* and *The New Republic*.

Little we do as individuals will matter much if we make the same mistakes as the liberal democrats of pre-Hitler Germany and Italy. If we lose the precious product of a struggle for free will that began only a few hundred years ago, no one will later ask us if we want it back.

The most necessary work of anyone who wishes to be free themselves is to protect the freedom of everyone around them. But constitutions, laws and courts offer no guarantees of this freedom. When the Supreme Court decided against the wishes of Andrew Jackson, the president reputedly said, "The court has made its decision, now let it enforce it." Judge Learned Hand argued that constitutions and such are false hopes: "Liberty lies in the hearts of men and women; when it dies there is no constitution, no law, no court that can save it."

We still act and talk as though we are the legitimate offspring of those who declared that we possessed certain inalienable rights. But increasingly, we are become only virtual descendants, finding comfort in seductive but ultimately useless symbolism.

Such as Visa's "free speech" web site where you could "express your opinions, place your vote, make your choices. See whether others agree . . . Vote your conscience, vote your mind." The questions, however, were ones such as how often do you read your horoscope and what's the most overexposed TV show.

Nadav Savio, whose father launched the free speech movement of the 1960s, argued on his own web site that Visa was "substituting brand preference for freedom of expression." Free speech, he argued, now means "little more than making consumer decisions." For corporate managers of our own brave new world — as with the military planners — you are the target.

The ultimate danger is the one of which Thomas Jefferson spoke when he warned that following the Revolution,

> It will not be necessary to resort every moment to the people for support. They will be forgotten, therefore, and their rights disregarded. They will forget themselves save in the sole faculty of making money, and will never think of uniting to effect a due respect for their rights. The shackles, therefore . . . will be made heavier and heavier, till our rights shall revive or expire in a convulsion.

Now it is our turn in history. We flip the page and see the ad: "Southwest Airlines. The symbol of Freedom."

And of a country that has forgotten what freedom really is.

FALSE PROFITS

One of the problems with living around powerful myths is that you can start to feel personally responsible when they don't work out. If you don't lose weight, have better sex, kick your phobia, earn 20% annually in the stock market, or get the job you want, there are few around to tell you that such outcomes are pretty normal. Instead, we are surrounded by hucksters of success and salvation constantly luring us towards illusory certainty. If we succumb to these chimeras of profit and prophecy, if we accept the idea that God rightly favors the successful, the economy justly favors the lucky, and society fairly favors the glamorous, it can ultimately leave us with a sense of failure for no greater fault than being a normal human being. It is hard in such a context to remember that nearly all people who dial the 900 number beckoning them on the cable screen continue to find hard times on easy street.

One of the greatest of our present myths is that a free market cures all ills. One would never guess from the commentators of NPR and PBS, for example, that if there were actually a free market in this country, they would be out of work, as would be the conservative economists and other welfare intellectuals sinecured at public universities. Thousands of Washington lawyer-lobbyists would also be unemployed, the defense industry would crash, and all the airports would have to close.

The truth is, as with every society that has ever existed, our economy is not only a conglomerate, but a part of, and dependent upon, a huge number of values, rules, systems, and characteristics that comprise a culture. We can no more isolate the use of money or labor from these factors than we could declare society to be henceforth based on free lunch.

Fortunately, economists discovered money as an organizing principle rather than, say, defecation. Otherwise, instead of the GDP, we would have to listen to Eleanor Clift or George Will pontificating on the latest trends in the Gross National Movement. Aside from avoiding that mishap, however, the monomaniacal obsession with the flow of money offers little in the way of insight. It is — there is really no better word — childish, for it simplifies reality into infantile dichotomies beyond all logic and evidence.

You need look no further than the free marketers themselves to see how false the notion of a free market is. Would a truly free market, for example, tolerate government officials with as much arbitrary power as the members of the Federal Reserve? Can one — as a matter of logic rather than economics — love both the Federal Reserve and a free market? Isn't monetarism really just a form of socialism that favors capitalists instead of workers?

Certainly, if one thing has *not* characterized the last two decades it has been any reluctance by our leaders to inject themselves into our lives. An era that has been devoted to the free market has simultaneously been the most governmentally intrusive in our history. In the name of a free market we have indentured ourselves to a system overflowing in other regards with contempt for personal liberty. In such ways, concepts such as the "market economy" and "monetarism" have gilded the lily of the very power they pretend to oppose. They provide a comfortable cover for what the government has really been about.

Peter Jay once noted that introducing the mother of new capitalism, Margaret Thatcher, to monetarism was like showing Genghis Kahn a map of the world. Thatcher had a mean and narrow view of life; she didn't even accept the existence of community, declaring once that "there is no such thing as society. There are individual men and women, and there are families." Thatcher wrapped herself in economic slogans that justified greed not only to accomplish economic ends but also to deal with gays and abortions and everything else she didn't like. In her paradigm, the free market and Victorian tyranny formed a civil union. By the time Reagan, two Bushes, and Clinton were through with the concept, they had created a gaping corporate exemption from common morality and decency. The market not only offered adequate justification for any act, it had replaced God as the highest source of law.

Until the Reagan-Bush-Clinton-Bush era it would have been next to impossible to find a culture that survived for long believing that the unfettered, rapacious flow of money and goods was the core of human existence. Elsewhere, to be sure, commerce had looked to bottom lines, but these had included those established by church, community, government, and tradition.

Of course it could be argued that the new capitalists, as single-factor fetishists, were no worse than Marxists. I know, for example, that I can usually stop an eruption of Marxist rhetoric for at least a few minutes by asking the simple question: who will run the restaurants in utopia? I find few people even on the hard left who wish to eat and drink the product of collectivism for the rest of their lives.

Marxists and capitalists share an obsession with money and a taste for clichéd mantras about it. They also share a willingness to reduce the complexity of human existence to just a couple of choices. Nonetheless, it makes more sense to devote our attention to the capitalists because they are doing a far better job of making everyone go along with them. And making us suffer in the process.

One of the reasons a free market is so hard to come by is because it has never existed. In modern times the drug trade comes closer in some respects than more legal activities, but even there mafias and murders interrupt the free flow of capital goods. The form of capitalism known as "free trade" doesn't even come close, else one wouldn't need 2,000-page agreements and the World Trade Organization. And we wouldn't have laws against usury and on behalf of workplace safety.

Besides, culture keeps interfering with the economists' theories. A foreign aid official once noticed that women in a certain third-world village had to row daily across a broad lake in order to reach the marketplace. Using the efficient analysis of first-world MBAs, it was determined that what these third-world women needed were some outboard motors.

And so motors were bought and distributed. Within a month or two, however, every one of them had fallen overboard. At which point, the aid official realized an important non-economic truth: the women actually liked rowing together across the lake, finding it a convivial, communal activity.

The idea that such factors as social mores or religious values take precedence over efficient cash flow did not really seem odd until the 1980s. The term capitalism wasn't even invented until the middle of the 19th century, and the early robber barons carried out their business without a manic need to justify their addictions publicly. Part of the earlier privilege of wealth was that no one had to know what you did with it. And it wasn't until the 1980s that the proselytizing of greed became so ubiquitous that even otherwise humble human beings began using words in ordinary conversation like *entrepreneur, bottom-line, strategic vision,* and *market-driven.*

Much of this language is not that of management, but of marketing. It is almost as if the ghost of Willy Loman had risen from the dead to exercise some supernatural vengeance on the nation. Not only is the salesman-hustler fully alive; he is all of us everywhere all the time — from the several thousand advertising messages we confront daily; to the hour each day we spend reading, hearing, or viewing them; to the 77 distinct images in one 60-second GE commercial; to the massive shift in the work day during which the production of propaganda has often replaced the production of products.

◆ ◆ ◆

But haven't we been repeatedly told that it all works out for the better in the end? Well, that isn't what Adam Smith thought. The patron saint of capitalism said in *Wealth of Nations* that "Consumption is the sole end and purpose of all production; and the interest of the producer ought to be attended to only so far as it may be necessary for promoting that of the consumers . . . In the mercantile system the interest of the consumer is almost constantly sacrificed to that of the producer; and it seems to consider production, and not consumption, as the ultimate end and object of all industry and commerce."

The state restraints and protectionism that bothered Smith were those that affected small business, not huge corporations. As David Korten notes, today's economic system "bears far greater resemblance to the monopolistic market system [Smith] condemned than it does to the theoretical competitive market system he hypothesized":

Adam Smith's ideal was a market comprised solely of small buyers and sellers, each too small to influence the market price of the commodities exchanged. Thus, Smith's concept of a competitive market was one in which there were no large business with monopolistic market powers . . . Smith was opposed to any kind of monopoly power . . . Adam Smith also assumed that investors have a natural preference for selling close to home. In other words, Adam Smith assumed that capital would be rooted in a particular place.

Nor can historical justification for the boomer barons be found in the history of our own country, though the "market economy" is often mentioned as though embedded in the Constitution. It is true that the American Revolution was an economic as well as a political victory, triumphing over a system in which only the nobility and a few large merchants held economic power. But the definition of economic freedom was quite different from that used by today's corporate chief executive seeking yet another tax break or a bigger bonus. Early free Americans widely believed that one was entitled to the "fruits of your labor" and no more. They opposed the concentration of property because it would allow property owners to seize political power.

There was already more than a little experience with this. Eric Foner points out that by 1770,

profits derived from slavery furnished up to a third of Britain's capital formation, and slave-grown products had became ubiquitous in England, emblems of a rising bourgeoisie and common even in the working class . . . Now, as then, commerce unrestrained by social control ends up stripping economic relations of all moral content, while the drive toward fulfilling market demands at the lowest possible price created widespread indifference to the conditions under which marketable goods are produced. Today's Chinatown sweatshops and Third World child labor factories are the functional equivalents of colonial slavery in that the demands of the consumer and the profit drive of the entrepreneur overwhelm the rights of those whose labor actually produces the salable commodity.

In America, by the time of the Civil War, slaves were the country's most valuable capital asset. In a nation with an annual federal budget of only $50 million, slaves had a market value of $2 billion, or more than twice that of all the country's railroads. That was not a free market.

◆ ◆ ◆

Further, the Constitution was written for non-slave Americans and not for corporations. Free enterprise was not mentioned in it. During the entire American colonial period only about a half-dozen business corporations were chartered. In the first 20 years after the Revolution only about 150 corporations were chartered. Each of these charters required that the corporation be in the public interest. Jefferson to the end opposed liberal grants of corporate charters and argued that states should be allowed to intervene in corporate matters or take back a charter if necessary.

These early Americans were, however, deeply commercial. One reason for this was that commercial activity allowed you to break free of the social and economic restrictions of a British economy based on nobility and monopoly. Americans didn't want to work for such a system; they wanted to work for themselves. And they weren't concerned about competition because there wasn't much.

With the pressure for more commerce, and growing indications that corporate grants were becoming a form of patronage, states began passing free incorporation laws and before long Massachusetts had 30 times as many corporations as there were in all of Europe. Still it wasn't until after the Civil War that economic conditions turned sharply in favor of the large corporation. These corporations, says historian James Huston:

> . . . killed the republican theory of the distribution of wealth
> and probably ended whatever was left of the political theory of
> republicanism as well. . . . [The] corporation brought about a
> new form of dependency. Instead of industry, frugality, and ini-
> tiatives producing fruits, underlings in the corporate hierarchy
> had to be aware of style, manners, office politics, and choice of
> patrons — very reminiscent of the Old Whig corruption in
> England at the time of the revolution — what is today called
> "corporate culture."

Concludes Huston:

> The rise of big business generated the most important transfor-
> mation of American life that North America has ever experi-
> enced.

It truly represented a counter-coup against the values of the American Revolution. It dramatically undermined both political and economic freedom, corrupted politicians and ransacked national assets. It replaced the feudalism of the monarchy with the feudalism of the corporation.

Perhaps the most important event occurred 110 years after the launching of the Revolution. In 1886, the Supreme Court ruled that a corporation was a person under the 14th Amendment and entitled to such constitutional protections as those of free speech.

With this fiction, the court helped to boost the corporate takeover of America. It helped personalize the corporation and depersonalize the individual, giving the former moral standing without moral responsibility, and making the human soul subservient to a soulless creation of the law.

As Morton Mintz pointed out, the court ignored the fact that "the only 'person' Congress had in mind when it adopted the 14th Amendment in 1866 was the newly freed slave." Justice Black observed in the 1930s that in the first 50 years following the adoption of the 14th Amendment, less than one-half of one percent of Supreme Court cases "invoked it in protection of the Negro race, and more than 50 percent asked that its benefits be extended to corporations." During this same period the courts moved to limit democratic power in other ways as well. For example, the Supreme Court restricted the common law right of juries to nullify a wrongful law; other courts erected barriers against third parties and banned fusion slates.

It was during this time that the myth of competitive virtue sprouted, helping to justify the rapaciousness of American business. It was a time when J.P. Morgan would come to own half the railroad mileage in the country — the same J. P. Morgan who got his start during the Civil War buying defective rifles for $3.50 each from an army arsenal and then selling them to a general in the field for $22 apiece. What we now proudly call the "American free market system," was initially propelled by slavery and flowered in an era of enormous bribes, massive legislative corruption, and great anti-competitive cartels. It was a time when the government, in a precursor to modern industrial policy, gave two railroad companies 21 million acres of free land.

It was also the time that American workers, who had once used commerce to free themselves from the economic and social straitjacket of feudalism, found themselves servants of a new rigid hierarchy, that of the modern corporation.

As persons, corporations could inject themselves fully into civic life (such as influencing campaigns and politicians) while still repelling public interference in their own affairs. They could construct barriers on civil liberties grounds against efforts to control their greed. Many of the rights that corporations secured by law came even as blacks and women were still struggling towards full enfranchisement.

The political movement of populism did battle with the new corporations but lost, as did the socialists who followed. Save during the Depression, generations of Americans would come to accept the myth of free enterprise. They did so in part because these companies provided higher incomes and ever-increasing jobs. But in the last quarter of the 20th century, these two conditions began to disappear. No small part of today's political tension stems from the rising power of big corporations even as their social and economic contribution to America declines.

For many years the free enterprise myth was countered by competing perspectives, but since the 1980s economists have firmly established themselves as the official judges of human progress, replacing such numerically challenged trades as philosophy, anthropology, religion, political science, and history. These economists have argued that we would be rewarded by economic growth when, in fact, the Reagan-Bush-Clinton era was one of unusually low growth, matched in the 20th century only in 1910–'19 and during the Depression. Here are some things, however, that have grown:

+ A subculture of narcissistic, avaricious, bullying, exploitative corporate cavaliers suffering from deep social dyslexia.
+ The false measurement of virtue, progress, success, and happiness by short-term economic markets that deny or devalue achievements or failure in other areas.
+ Commercial viruses, a.k.a. advertising, that hack into our visual and aural space as effectively as a computer hacker invades a web site.

Even workers, though, have come to accept the free market mythology. As Sister Souljah said, "They think that if they're not doing all right they're an individual failure. They can no longer draw the relationship between their lack of success and the system which is set up for them to be unsuccessful."

Richard Sennett in *The Corrosion of Character* pinpoints some of the personal consequences of work under the new capitalism:

+ THE END OF LONG-TERM WORK. A young American today with at least two years of college can expect to change jobs at least 11 times in the course of working, and "change his or her skill base at least three times during those 40 years of labor." . . . "'Jobs' are being replaced by 'projects' and 'fields of work.'" Says Sennett, "Promotions and dismissals tend not to be based on clear, fixed rules, nor are work tasks crisply defined." One of the consequences of this approach is that it "corrodes trust, loyalty, and mutual commitment."
+ TECHNOLOGY LIMITS PERSONAL CONTROL. Under the old capitalism even dull and routine work typically required some level of individual control over a machine, such as understanding how to get it running again when it broke down. The desire for such mastery hasn't disappeared. For example, Katherine Newman, in a study of servers at McDonald's restaurants, found that these workers quickly sprung into action when something went wrong. This was

not the case, however, when a machine broke down at a modern bakery that Sennett studied: "Though simple to use, the dough-kneading machine was complex in design; its computer operating system was opaque, as industrial designers say, rather than transparent . . . The electricity was shut off, a telephone call was made, and we sat for two hours waiting for the service saviors to arrive from the firm which had designed the machines . . . Once the plug was pulled on the electricity, the waiting workers were morose and upset . . . The bakers were not indifferent to the elemental fact of getting a job done. They wanted to be helpful, to make things work, but they couldn't."

+ A MISLEADING LANGUAGE that, among other things, encourages risk without outlining the nature of that risk. Business books use comfortable images such as a gardener's "repotting" to explain the lack of stability in the modern corporation. The key fact one needs to know about risk – but which isn't explained in the new capitalism – is that your chances of getting a second full house in poker are exactly the same as they were in the previous hand, which is to say not very good. The same principle works when moving to a new job. One study even found that your chances of "moving up" in such a shift were less than if you stayed at the old job.

+ THE FREE MARKET ENDS AT 55. The number of men aged 54–65 still in the workplace dropped from nearly 80% in 1970 to 65% in 1990. The rate of involuntary dismissal has doubled in the last 20 years for men in their 40s to early 50s. Combined with a later age at which the young become significantly employed, this has greatly narrowed the life span of individual usefulness.

+ A FALSE SENSE OF COOPERATION AND TEAMWORK: It is popular for firms to refer to their employees as "partners," "associates," or "team members." Among the results, Sennett observes, is to lessen management's responsibility; it is, after all, only "coaching" the team. Such language also makes it difficult, "if not fatal," as Laurie Graham found in her study of a Subaru-Isuzu plant, "for a worker to talk straight to a boss-coach about problems in terms other than team cooperation; straight talk involving demands for higher pay or less pressure to boost productivity was seen as a lack of employee cooperativeness. The good team player doesn't whine."

◆ THE NEW CAPITALISM HAS GREATLY EXPANDED THE POTEN-
TIAL FOR FAILURE. The winner-take-all market is a competitive structure which makes it easy for large numbers of
educated people to fail. Down-sizings and re-engineerings
impose sudden disasters on middle class people which in
traditional capitalism were mainly confined to lower
classes.

◆ ◆ ◆

Such strains put a burden on workers that is generally underrated. A 1999
British study found that employers could expect to lose two out of five workers
as a direct result of too much pressure. Nearly one in three employees reported
health strains, and more than one in four said their sex life had suffered because
of their work. The biggest complaints:

◆ Work unappreciated by superiors
◆ Inability to balance work and home life
◆ Too much stress
◆ Too much work

Managers fared no better. A contemporaneous survey by the British publi-
cation, *Management Today*, found that 55% of manager respondents felt frequently stressed at work and 50% said they were too busy to create proper
relationships outside of the office.

As with so many aspects of our lives, we are stymied in addressing such problems in part because our culture frowns on those who confront them. Even in
such elite corners of information as book reviews and public broadcasting, we
find a cultured ignorance perpetuating the deceptions of the corporate world.
After all, if NPR thinks we live in an "free market democracy," who are we to
argue? If Jim Lehrer is willing to explain patiently and somberly the wonders of
multinationalism, who are we to point out that one of his major corporate
underwriters paid a record $100 million fine for international price fixing?

This conspiracy of silence also dumps down the memory hole the problems
of the non-college educated, the farmer, small businesses (which produce most
of the new jobs in this country), young males, and those otherwise not qualified for capitalistic celebration. It slides over massive criminality by corporations. It ignores the fact that American business grew faster during the rise of
the labor movement than it did after it learned how to suppress unions. It
ignores the true variety of economic systems that can exist in favor of a trite and
false dichotomy between capitalism and socialism.

Such distortions can have profound consequences. The collapse of the
Russian economy following the breakup of the Soviet Union was due, in no

small part, to extraordinary exploitation by western "free market" advocates, assisted by an absurdly low valuation of the country's financial assets. It was said that the Russian stock market was the cheapest place in the world to drill for oil and natural gas.

Russian expert Stephen Cohen of New York University would later remark, "It may be that President Gorbachev's much-scorned gradualism and goal of a mixed economy, based on combining marketization and privatization with whatever was viable in the old state system, were (and may still be) the best way to reform Russia, and other Soviet republics."

Neither is America stuck with rigid economic models that have caused so much individual and aggregate pain. There are all sorts of mixed economies. There are big consumer cooperatives like Land o' Lakes Butter and the United Services Automobile Association that have thrived happily amongst conventional capitalists. The town of Green Bay, Wisconsin, holds its professional football team in community ownership. As a result, it's one of the few professional sports teams in America that we know won't be moving to someplace else. There are various forms of local currency, including "time dollars" with which people earn time credits that can be redeemed in services.

Perhaps most significantly, we prove again and again the limits and liabilities of promiscuous capitalism by personal actions that mitigate its evils and compensate for its failures. Every labor union, every act of charity, every anti-sweatshop group, every barter, every voluntary activity for the good of the community, every code of conduct that defines the morality of commerce, every deal foregone for reasons of decency, every time someone does something for someone and says, "think nothing of it," is a revolt against the Church of False Profits.

The impact of these non-capitalistic activities can be enormous. Nike sales dropped 27% after news of the company's sweatshop practices were widely circulated. The Trends Report of 1997 found three out of four customers willing to switch equal quality brands if one is associated with a good cause. A *Business Week* survey found that 95% of Americans don't think a corporation should only exist to make money. A report published in *Management Accounting* found that "one investment dollar out of every ten is placed with ethical or social criteria in mind."

Further evidence of the options available can be found by comparing cultures. For example, in *American Exceptionalism*, Seymour Lipset cites an eight year study of 15,000 managers and executives in six countries in which 40% of the Americans agreed that "the only real goal of a company is making a profit," while only 8% of the Japanese managers felt the same way. All but one percent of the Americans expected that their employment at a company would be of limited duration, while a majority of the Japanese thought they would be employed at their companies for life. And while 85% of the Japanese believed that the best way to pick someone for a position was to meet and discuss the selection until almost everyone had agreed on someone, only 38% of Americans felt that way, preferring a simple majority vote.

◆ ◆ ◆

Even in this country there are many companies that have offered alternatives to the compulsive, controlling, and often corrupt capitalism so often used as the desirable prototype. Three frequently cited are L.L. Bean, Tom's of Maine Soap, and Ben & Jerry's. Interestingly, each began in New England in a culture with a long tradition of respect for the individual and for integrity in personal dealings. The companies shared an understanding that business is just one part of life that must be integrated with all the others. Of course, such behavior is not purely altruistic. Traditions of fair-dealing survive because they work well for everyone, including the company. Besides, the Reagan-Bush-Clinton years took their toll on L.L. Bean which, like so many other large corporations, began hyping the image of what it is supposed to be even as the reality behind the image was fading.

Bean's problems began in part when the company hired some Boston consultants in 1998 who advised it to "restructure" the corporate offices into "eight strategic business units" such as L.L. Home, L.L. Kids, and L.L. Sports. The firm also suggested a number of other moves popular with contemporary techno-managers. Soon, however, the company found itself also faced with a major unionization effort by the Teamsters.

According to Lisa Chmelecki of the *Falmouth Forecaster* newspaper

> "[The Boston Consulting Group] assigned managers to each unit and they told everyone that they had to reapply for their jobs," said one employee who had worked there for 15 years. According to Kayser [a former employee] and the others, almost every corporate employee had to submit a resume and one-page essay describing their aspirations as an L.L. Bean employee. They also had to submit a list indicating the positions for they were applying.
>
> "All work stopped for at least three months," Kayser said. "Nothing got done, because we were all printing off resumes and were being encouraged to spend time meeting with the managers who would be hiring us . . . "
>
> "I never even had to write a resume before," [another ex-employee] said." There was so much pressure to prove ourselves, to go around strutting our stuff. My record should have spoken for itself. . . . L.L. Bean is not the company I went to work for six years ago. The attitude has changed. Now, it is strictly about numbers. People are dispensable."

[Another worker told Chmelecki] "There was a time when
L.L. Bean talked to the [employees] before making any major
changes and there were management people that looked after
the little guy — not so today."

Such changes reflect the corrosive effects of the new capitalism and some of
the bizarre management techniques that have accompanied it. These changes,
according to one survey, found 56% of employees nationally saying their
company did not genuinely care about them and a similar percentage saying
that they have no strong loyalty towards their firm.

In the end, L.L. Bean avoided unionization after giving employees some of
the benefits that a union would have sought and Bean itself might have offered
without prompting in an earlier time. Bonuses, not seen for five years, were
resumed and employees were granted additional holiday time off, night-time
premium pay, a relaxation in the dress code, and a fitness program.

Another company that, until it was sold, provided an alternative model
was Ben & Jerry's. In 1992, Ben & Jerry's sales jumped 36% while profits
rose 79%. Early that year Ben Cohen wrote a letter to shareholders in which
he said:

The most amazing thing is that our social values — that part of
our company mission statement that calls us to use our power
as a business to improve the quality of life in our local, national
and international communities — have actually helped us to
become a stable, profitable, high-growth company. This is especially interesting because it flies in the face of those business theorists who state that publicly held corporations cannot make a
profit and help the community at the same time, and moreover
that such companies have no business trying to do so.

Needless to say, some business observers remained skeptical, especially when
Ben decided to take a six-month sabbatical. *Forbes* ran an article in March 1992
reporting that Ben had quit as CEO after coming down with "a bad case of the
guilties" over the company's financial success. The day the magazine hit the
streets, the company's stock lost 10 percent of its value. By November, however,
Forbes had to admit that B&J was still on its list of the 200 best small companies in America — for the third year in a row.

Another New England businessman, Tom Chappell of Maine, started a
natural ingredient toothpaste firm in 1974 with a $5,000 loan and a few
investors. By 1981 his firm was doing $1.5 million in sales and has been going
strong ever since.

A few years later, however, Chappell found himself telling a minister friend,
"I'm tired of creating new brands and making money."

In his book, *Soul of Business*, Chappell recalls, "I had never thought such a sentence would come out of me. But there I was, asserting that though I was very successful, I felt empty."

Chappell's remarkable solution was to go to Harvard Divinity School. He returned later, not only revived, but with theologian Richard Niebuhr in tow. He gathered his board — including a business school dean and a Washington lawyer — to listen to Niebuhr and discuss their assigned reading, Martin Buber's *I and Thou*. After the talk, the board broke up into small groups, augmented by staff members and local ministers, to discuss "how we might apply Buber's ideas to our lives and business practices." The Washington lawyer later told Chappell, "This was the most exciting thing I've done in a long time."

To Chappell the message was:

> Beliefs drive strategy. Your ethics can form the foundation of smart analysis and clear thinking. Your personal values can be integrated with managing for all the traditional goals of business. . . . You can be a hard-ass competitor and still run a business with a soul. . . .

◆ ◆ ◆

Having spent considerable time in Maine, such things don't really surprise me. After all, I once bought a used car sight unseen over the phone from R&D Automotive in Freeport because I figured I'd do better that way that shopping around at Washington area lots. The 1983 Chevy station wagon got both my sons back and forth to college and made two and half trips across the country.

From childhood on I have run into traits that, while not unique to Maine nor universal in Maine, were nonetheless in considerably greater supply there than in many other places. I make no claim as to the persistence of these traits nor do I to wish to romanticize them. After all, when I first went to Maine as an eight-year-old there were four times as many acres in farmland as there are today and much else has disappeared as well. Still, certain Maine values have floated on the surface of my experience like lobster buoys off the starboard bow. Among them:

> ◆ INTEGRITY: Integrity is not just honesty but a quality in which all the parts fit together. Watertight integrity on a ship, for example, means that the bulkheads are not three feet thick in one place and rusted out elsewhere. Today those at the top often undervalue completeness, consistency, reliability — preferring the momentary impact, the single-minded pursuit, the exceptional event.

♦ COMMUNITY: Contrary to current mythology, community traditionally has had a great impact on the nature of business. Today's rhetoric denies it a place and derides those who advocate it as "community activists," as if maintaining the social compact was some sort of revolutionary act. I once observed the conflict between old and new ways of business at a meeting in a small Maine town. The CEO of a chain of boat yards had flown up from Connecticut to tell the community why his firm could not save a 19th century building that was the last link with the town's shipbuilding past. The evening progressed as such debates do until a young contractor arose and spoke directly to the CEO. He earnestly explained how, in a small town, business was done in a different way. Everyone was connected to everyone else. Then he added, "I work knowing that if I do a bad job on a house, somebody is going to tell my parents about it." Can you imagine Michael Eisner or Steve Case saying that?

♦ RESPECT: The prevalence of independent farmers, craftspeople, the fishing industry, and small business — and the absence of plantation agriculture and relative lack of industrial capitalism — helped to create a culture of respect and a flattened social hierarchy. Authority grew out of competence and reputation, not power. Maine humor, interestingly, centers on the foolish acts of the powerful stranger compared to the less powerful but wiser native.

♦ COOPERATION. The relationship between farmers or fishing boat captains defies the simplistic competitive rules of capitalist economics. Yes, there is competition, but at the same time there is an unusual degree of cooperation, described well by anthropologist James Acheson in *The Lobster Gangs of Maine*:

The relevant social unit for most fisherman is not the fishing industry as a whole; it is the men fishing for the same species with the same gear in the same area. They share skills and a common knowledge of the means to exploit and market a certain product . . . Although they are direct competitors, lobstermen are the most useful people in one another's lives . . . The men in each gang are involved in an elaborate dance-like interaction in which cooperation must be balanced with competition, secrecy with openness, and sharing with self-interest.

♦ ECOLOGICAL WISDOM: One can not spend much time in
Maine without learning what Barry Commoner called the
four lessons of ecology:

Everything is connected to everything else
Everything must go somewhere
Nature knows best
There is no such thing as a free lunch.

In Washington and corporate America, on the other hand,
the environment is treated as just another special interest
group with which to negotiate, to ignore if you can, and to
appease as cheaply as possible if you can't.

♦ Self-reliance and appreciation of the real. My time in
Maine has been graced by an extraordinary number of men
and women who practiced the art of self reliance. I was
taught how to get through hurricanes, how to move a
house on skids, how to jack up a barn — all before I even
got to college. I am reminded of the importance of simple
skill and effort each time I look at the loose stones still
holding a 100 year-old barn upright. On the other hand,
when I return to Washington, all around me I find people
who deeply believe that words can substitute for competence. It doesn't work.

♦ ♦ ♦

My sense of commerce as a part of the holistic web of culture has also been
strengthened by having had a Quaker education. It has been said that the
Quakers came to this country to do good and did very well. This was not only
a matter of choice, it was a necessity. As with so many later immigrants, commerce was part of the escape route to freedom and a better life.

The values espoused by Quakers — particularly trustworthiness — served
them well in business. In both England and America it helped lead to major
accumulations of wealth. A descendent of a prominent Quaker thinker established Barclay's Bank; the Quaker Lloyd family built another of England's "big
five" financial institutions; and the Cadburys started a chocolate firm.

Being a fairly literate and conscientious crowd, Quaker entrepreneurs left a
useful paper trail of reflection, self-justification, and remorse on the question of
blending commerce and conscience. A common theme was the one laid out
early by George Fox:

There is the danger and temptation to you of drawing your minds into your business, and clogging them with it; so that ye can hardly do any thing to the service of God, but there will be crying my business, my business!

In 1839, John Sargent fretted:

On going to my brickfield I was thoughtful as to my partnership with Cardiot, and that my wood-burning business alone might be sufficient to me, and perhaps more to my spiritual advantage than being too much cumbered with business.

Martha Routh, whose school had outgrown its quarters, also worried about mergers and acquisitions. She visited a possible new site:

As I passed from room to room I was attended by a secret but clear intimation that I was not to entangle myself with a greater number of scholars than the house we already had would accommodate, so I entirely gave up the thought and found peace.

David Ferris, in 1855, was concerned about the rum he was selling:

Being unwilling to lose the profits of this branch of business, I adopted an expedient to soothe my pain; which was to refuse selling it to such as I thought would make evil use of it. But this did not answer my expectations; for they would send for it by those who were not suspected. At length I was made to relinquish the profits made on this article; and trust to Providence for the result. [Which, it turned out, made "no great diminution" of his business.]

As Quaker businesses grew they carried their traditions with them. The big English firms of Cadbury, Fry and Rowntree built whole communities for their workers and, in America, Quaker firms even welcomed the idea of unions. Writes Robert Lawrence Smith:

Quaker businessmen recognized that unions were essential as a means of communication between management and workers. Many saw collective bargaining at its best as similar to the search for consensus that goes on at Quaker meetings for business. Viewed this way, negotiations become a method for bringing about an enlightened resolution or synthesis of different points of view. One result is that, by and large, workers at Quaker businesses have been able to reach fair contract terms without resorting to strikes.

As late as 1951, a British Quaker industrialist addressed his colleagues this way:

> The greatest source of waste arises through lack of cordial coop-eration between employers and employed. Our aim should be to induce all to work as hard and as intelligently as if they were working for themselves . . . Remember, there is no such thing as "labor." The working force is made up of a number of individ-uals each having a personality different from the rest. They are sensitive as we are to encouragement and discouragement, as easily aroused to anger and suspicion, to loyalty and to effort.

Did the speaker's words conceal certain hypocrisies or perhaps represent paternalism parading as equality? It is not unlikely. But the question is not whether Quaker business people lived up to their professions of conscience but whether such professions positively affected the nature of their businesses. History strongly suggests that they did and that personal witness in the marketplace worked better for customer, worker, and owner than did an economy unnagged by conscience. Actions are seldom better than the beliefs that drive them.

We live in a time that attempts to deny this, that wishes to give commerce alone an exemption from all the moral and philosophical constraints that help to define a decent culture. This is done with the help of fraudulent computations of the market's worth and by imputing efficiency to what is merely greed.

Here, rather than in theoretical arguments over neatly dichotomized economies that have not and will not exist, should be our central question about commerce. What has traditionally kept commerce on track has been a complex network of social controls and individual conscience. Not just competition but the fact that the owner of the small town bank belonged to the same church as his customers. Not market share but a fair market. Not just a new customer base but customers you had to face.

Far too many have suffered from the self-serving dicta of the new capitalism, which replaced the Bill of Rights with the commerce clause. The counterfeit economy has served none of us well, not even those who have been its strongest advocates. For example, Robert Kurzon, a 1990 graduate of that corporate aux-iliary, the Harvard Law School, interviewed his classmates for *Esquire* and found "those who have left law, especially law firms, seem happy. Those who have not are suffering, or, worse, resigned. They talk about losing themselves. These are strange times in the workplace, and one need only look to Harvard

Law School for an example." A number were even afraid to talk to him for fear of losing their jobs. Said one, "I hope you find someone who will talk — God knows there's enough of us suffering out there." Said another, "My dream is to become a clerk at Barnes & Noble . . . I've got the store picked out. I literally fantasize about this." Among those who did escape, one ended up as a comedian and another shifted his practice to represent taxi drivers in traffic court.

Behind much of this angst is an economy that has separated even its own practitioners from the support, sense, discipline, and integrity that comes from blending one's ambitions and values with those of others and from knowing and accepting that in economics, as in ecology, there is still no free lunch.

DESPAIR and SURVIVAL

ALL THROUGH MY BOYHOOD I HAD A PROFOUND CONVIC-
TION THAT I WAS NO GOOD, THAT I WAS WASTING MY TIME,
WRECKING MY TALENTS, BEHAVING WITH MONSTROUS FOLLY
AND WICKEDNESS AND INGRATITUDE — AND ALL THIS, IT
SEEMED, WAS INESCAPABLE, BECAUSE I LIVED AMONG LAWS
WHICH WERE ABSOLUTE, LIKE THE LAW OF GRAVITY, BUT
WHICH IT WAS NOT POSSIBLE FOR ME TO KEEP. . . . BUT THIS
SENSE OF GUILT AND INEVITABLE FAILURE WAS BALANCED BY
SOMETHING ELSE; THAT IS, THE INSTINCT TO SURVIVE. EVEN
A CREATURE THAT IS WEAK, UGLY, COWARDLY, SMELLY AND IN
NO WAY JUSTIFIABLE STILL WANTS TO STAY ALIVE AND BE
HAPPY UNDER ITS OWN FASHION.

George Orwell in *"Such, Such were the Joys. . ."*

Orwell, a lower income boy in an upscale British public school, found himself alone, without mentor, parent, or therapist. Instead he faced "the schoolmasters with their canes, the millionaires with their Scottish castles, the athletes with their curly hair — these were the armies of the unalterable law. It was not easy, at that date, to realize that in fact it was alterable. And according to that law I was damned."

Orwell went to school in another place and another time, but nearer and more recent is a school in Littleton, Colorado, where 13 youths were killed by a pair of fellow students. "Far from being a united, happy bunch," wrote the *London Guardian* afterwards, "Columbine students operated a fiercely regimented social hierarchy":

> There were the jocks, principally the football team, regarded by the rest as being allowed to operate as a law unto themselves by the school authorities. There were the preppies, the rich kids, despised by their peers because of a perception that they could buy their way through life. There were the skateboard punks, the cool kids envied for their street style. And, right at the bottom of the food chain, there were the students who could not fit into any of the other groups, the quiet, brooding, intelligent ones . . . These pupils were invariably shunned by the other tribes, and frequently bullied, verbally and physically.

Sara Rimer in the *New York Times* found something similar:

> The "individuals" shun the Gap and Abercrombie & Fitch, the
> labels favored by the jocks and preppies. [Jessica] would not be
> able to afford the $30 shirts and $25 hats even if she liked them.
> . . . "One jock has a Hummer," Jessica said. "He totaled one
> Hummer, and his dad bought him another.". . .

Susan Greene in the *Denver Post* quoted an anonymous 18-year-old who said
he was taunted and terrorized by his schoolmates,

> so-called jocks who called him "faggot," bashed him into
> lockers and threw rocks at him from their cars while he rode his
> bike home from school . . . Jocks would "speed past at 40, 50
> mph" and toss pop cans or cups full of sticky soda at him.
> Sometimes they threw rocks or even sideswiped his bike with
> their cars . . . In the cafeteria, he continued, jocks threw mashed
> potatoes at him.

Long before cable TV and fashion magazines and high school students
driving Hummers, the idea of an ideal lured Americans like sirens calling from
the ledge. Tocqueville caught it early:

> Among democratic nations men easily attain a certain equality
> of condition., but they never can attain as much as they desire.
> It perpetually retires from before them, yet without hiding itself
> from their sight, and in retiring draws them on. They are near
> enough to see its charms, but too far off to enjoy them; and
> before they have fully tasted its delights, they die.

Long before MTV and chicken dressed in 16 herbs, there was an industrial
revolution and in its wake, said Erich Fromm, man created a "world of man-
made things as it never existed before. He has constructed a complicated social
machine to administer the technical machine he built. The more powerful and
gigantic the forces are which he unleashes, the more powerless he feels himself
as a human being. He is owned by his own creation, and has lost ownership of
himself."

Long before Prozac and Ritalin and ecstasy there was soma, the drug of
choice in Aldous Huxley's *Brave New World*. Long before global eavesdropping
by the National Security Agency there was *1984*.

Yet something seems different. For example, suicide rates among the young
have risen for four decades. Between 1980 and 1996, the suicide rate for young
black men increased 105% and there has been a similar leap in suicides by all

children between 10 and 14. According to one calculation, more than 1.5 million young people under 15 are seriously depressed.

Kay Redfield Jamison, a leading researcher on suicide, tells of a 1997 study that found fully one in five high school students considering killing themselves in the past year. School slayings — though peaking in 1992–93 and but a fraction of youths murdered by members of their own families — reflect a change as well. In earlier years, reported the *New York Times*, most of these deaths were gang-related, or were stabbings, or involved money or a fight over a girlfriend. Towards the end of the decade, the motive changed. According to Dr. Bill Reisman, who profiles youth behavior for law enforcement officials, the most common factor was deep depression: "They'll all have depression in the state in which they do these things. When they're cornered, the first thing they say is, 'Kill me.' It's suicide by cop."

A study of 2,000 young men and women found 43% saying that they sometimes are pushed too far and feel like they might explode. And 58% of this group said they would use a gun "if they had to." The authors of the study, Liz Nickles and Laurie Ashcraft, observed that most people assume that "violent tendencies are the result of hands-off parenting." But, Nickles told the *New York Times*, "In the population we studied the opposite is the case. And Ashcraft added, "Over-scheduled, pressured children are an emotional powder keg."

When the worst happens, the "adult" reaction is typically to expand our automated distrust of the young. Politicians and the media often deal with public tragedies as though they were endemic rather than exceptions. Instead of reconciliation and comprehension, we demand still more control. But it never works quite the way we think it will, in part because the solutions are aimed at specific acts rather than the culture and problems that bred them. Thus we add surveillance cameras and guards at schools, and in so doing increase the sense of repression, distrust, and disconnection from the adult world that helped create the problem in the first place.

Corey Lyons, writing in the youth e-zine, *Brat*, described it this way:

> So here's what we have: kids who are constantly feeling repressed. They feel like the world is out to get them. Everything from school to television to church tells them they aren't good enough, that they are the problem. Then at school they face the same accusations of inadequacy by the self-righteous cliques that revel in our culture's mundane standards. The world suppresses their feelings until they feel they have no choice but to explode.

Or withdraw. At the start of the '90s, 40% of freshmen said that keeping up to date with political affairs was important. By 1998 only 27% said so. The number of freshmen participating in student elections dropped from 77% in

1968 to 21% three decades later. 36% said they are frequently bored in class, up 10 points from 1985. 26% say their parents were either divorced or not living together, three times more than when first asked in 1972.

And it's not just the young. Over half of Americans in 1996 saw a strong or moderate decline in the quality of television and entertainment, moral and ethical standards, family life, education and schools, the quality of our national leaders, our health care system, the work ethic, and our standard of living. In not a single area did more than a quarter of those responding see moderate or strong improvements. Worse, more and more Americans seem incapable of imagining life any other way or the possibility that they might have a role in making it otherwise. They have become passive consumers of their own demise.

Though we may concur in the critique, we don't know what to do about it and we don't know how to do it or whom to do it with. And as we struggle, all around us are shops with beautiful goods, photographs with beautiful bodies, politicians with beautiful policies, and the repetitive assurance that everything is all right. If we see it otherwise, it becomes our problem.

As our problem, we are quickly guided to beautiful solutions — to glib self-help literature, to multi-point nostrums, towards the smug assurance by the protected and entitled as they offer counsel to those who have never known a true triumph. This is America. If you can't make it, it's your own fault.

Even if you achieve a reputation for individuality, it becomes quickly stereotyped and you are expected to manifest your eccentricities in comfortably familiar and predictable ways. Avant-garde composer John Cage once said that whenever he did anything new, people just wanted him to keep doing it over and over again. And Cage, unlike famous rock musicians, didn't even have to contend with tens of thousands of fans in a stadium, an omnipresent media, and a cornucopia of temptations making plenty as difficult as scarcity.

Kurt Cobain sang, "I feel stupid and contagious . . . Here we are now, entertain us." When he was 12, "I wanted to be a rock and roll star, and I thought that would be my payback to all of the jocks who got girlfriends all of the time. But I realized way before I became a rock star that was stupid." Years later Cobain saw the payback as even less appealing:

> I think of myself as a success because I still haven't compromised my music, but that's just speaking on an artistic level. Obviously, all the other parts that belong with success are just driving me insane. What I really can't stand about being successful is when people confront me and say, 'Oh, you should just mellow out and enjoy it." I don't know how many times I have to fucking say this: I never wanted it in the first place.

And in his suicide note, he wrote:

Sometimes I feel as if I should have a punch-in time clock
before I walk out on stage

Cobain was far from alone. Here are some other musicians, many compiled
by Michael Woodall, who killed themselves or died of drug-induced causes.
Not included are those who died in airplane crashes or under disputed circum-
stances, who were murdered, or as in the case of Keith Relf, lead singer for the
Yardbirds, were electrocuted while playing an electric guitar through a 220-watt
Marshall amp while taking a bubble bath:

> Johnny Ace, Chris Acland, John Belushi, Mike Bloomfield,
> Tommy Bolin, Graham Bond, John Bonham, Adrian Borland,
> Roy Buchannan, Tim Buckley, Paul Butterfield, Glen Buxton,
> David Byron, Steve Clarke, Kurt Cobain, Ian Curtis, Nick
> Drake, Tom Evans, Peter Farndon, Bobby Fuller, Danny
> Gatton, Lowell George, Ric Grech, Pete Ham, Donny
> Hathaway, Bob "The Bear" Hite, James Honeyman-Scott,
> Shannon Hoon, Douglas Hopkins, Randy Jo Hobbs, Michael
> Hutchence, Robert Johnson, Billy Jones, Brian Jones, Janis
> Joplin, Paul Kossoff, Frankie Lymon, Richard Manuel, Robbie
> McIntosh, Joe Meek, Jonathan Melvoin, Keith Moon, Billy
> Murcia, Brent Mydland, Bradley Nowell, Phil Ochs, Brian
> O'Hara, Gram Parsons, Kristen Pfaff, Danny Rapp, Bon Scott,
> Del Shannon, Mel Street, Screaming Lord Sutch, Gary Thain,
> Johnny Thunders, E. William Tucker, Sid Vicious, Paul
> Williams, Rozz Williams, Wendy O. Williams, Kevin
> Wilkinson, Alan "Blind Owl" Wilson.

These were voices with whom contemporary youth on both sides of the
Atlantic grew up. Their average age at time of self-inflicted death: 34.1 years.
Cobain sang, "Gonna do it gonna die/Slowly, lonely, holy, lonely."
Somebody quoted Nine Inch Nails on a Nirvana web bulletin board, "I hurt
myself today to see if I still feel. I focus on the pain, the only thing that's real."
And Marilyn Manson told a Milwaukee newspaper, "I try to show people that
everything is a lie — pick the lie you like best — and I hope mine is the best."

◆ ◆ ◆

Ever since I read Thoreau in high school and adopted as my own his declaration that he would rather sit alone on a pumpkin than be crowded on a velvet
stool, I have made the pursuit of individual freedom a part of my daily business. I follow it like others follow football. I know the game, the players, and
the rules. And one of the most important things I have discovered is how few

people are able to help you much. The psychiatrist with his elegant degree, the minister with an eye on the vestry's budget, the philosophy professor just short of tenure, and, yes, even the author of this book are likely to fail because their work has become partly the suppression of their own free will.

This compromise may in the end represent a better balance of desire and action than that of which you dream, but it will not necessarily guide you well. It will not teach you how to do something even though you are afraid, even though no one else is suggesting that you do it let alone making you do it; it will not tell you when to take the risk of doing the right thing or trying something that no one has done before.

Which may be why one of the wisest observations on this subject came to me from a former LA narcotics detective. This detective, investigating corruption and involvement by intelligence agencies in the drug trade, has repeatedly put his life at risk to get to the bottom of an extremely dirty business. He has two bullet holes in his left arm and one in his left ear. While describing his efforts to a small group, someone asked how he managed to stick at it year after year despite having been shot and threatened. He said he had borrowed a trick another cop had taught him; when in danger he simply considered himself already dead. Then he was able to move without fear.

Such an ability to confront and transcend — rather than deny, adjust to, replace, recover from, or succumb to — the universe in which you find yourself is among the things that permits freedom. This man, with Buddhist-like deconstruction and Christian-like rebirth, had taken apart the pieces of his fear and dumped them on the ground — a mercy killing of dreams and nightmares on behalf of survival.

Yet imagine the health column in your local paper suggesting that you cure your phobia by going about pretending you are dead. Or phoning your psychiatrist in the middle of the night and having her tell you, "Just do the drop-dead thing I told you about and call me in the morning."

There is something almost perverse and subversive about the idea; like playing Russian roulette with your brain. One of the rules of our culture is not to let our minds come too close to death.

Albert Camus, on the other hand, claimed that the only serious philosophical question is suicide. Of this provocation, Christopher Scott Wyatt has written:

> According to Camus, suicide was a sign that one lacked the strength to face "nothing." Life is an adventure without final meaning, but still worth experiencing. Since there is nothing else, life should be lived to its fullest and derive meaning from human existence.
>
> Kierkegaard said that "the more consciousness, the more intense the despair," and that the torment of despair is not

being able to die. But lurking in this death wish, paradoxically, is a passion for life. If one survives this perilous proximity of death, one consciously chooses life.

But just what has been chosen? Certainly not a pristine and puerile Pleasantville of the soul. Perhaps it is what one of Camus' characters says: "I have surrendered myself to the magnificent indifference of the universe." Or perhaps we make Kierkegaard's "leap of faith," of which Donald Palmer wrote:

> The negative is present in all consciousness. Doubt accentuates the negative. Belief chooses to cancel the negative. Every mortal act is composed of doubt and belief . . . It is belief that sustains thought and holds the world together. Nevertheless, belief understands itself as uncertain, as not justified by any objective fact.

It is, in the end, your choice. Take a leap of faith and end up at the local church hoping someone can explain all this better to your kids in Sunday school than you can, or ride bareback across the philosophical and theological plains. In either case, as long as you fully engage with life, doubt will not be far away.

◆ ◆ ◆

The next witness is Corporal Gary Schluter of the Florida Highway Patrol. He has worked the Sunshine Skyway Bridge across Tampa Bay where his tasks included stopping people from killing themselves. He had little formal training, but over a three year period he and his colleagues helped to save over half the 53 people who tried to jump. In one instance, after talking for 40 minutes to a would-be jumper sitting on the rail of the bridge, legs over the side, the man said, "Gary, I'm really sorry, but I really have to go." Schluter and another officer inched close, finally near enough to gently lay a hand on the man's leg. "That's what I needed," the man said and came down off of the wall. Just a touch.

Schluter's partner, James Covert, told the *New York Times'* Rick Bragg, "I believe that everyone who goes up there has the intention of going through with it. They feel they've exhausted their options, and this is the last part of their lives they have control of. I tell them this is a permanent solution to a temporary problem."

In fact, a study done of attempted suicides on the Golden Gate Bridge — where 1,200 have jumped to their deaths over six decades — found that those who survive rarely try it a second time. As Emerson said, "We learn geology the day after the earthquake."

Happily, there is only one suicide each year for every 9,000 people in this country. There is less than a one in a million chance a student will be murdered on campus. Twice as many people were killed by lightning in 1997 as died in such incidents.

Still, about a half million Americans are treated in emergency rooms each year after trying to kill themselves. And as the suicide rate of people over 50 decreased in recent decades, the adolescent suicide rate almost tripled between 1960 and 1990. Further, the ratio of attempted to achieved suicides may be as much as 20 times higher for the young than for adults.

If one comes down off the bridge (metaphorical or real) and resumes endlessly pushing the stone up the hill so it can roll back down again, you find yourself once more living with the inexplicable, the insoluble, the absurd. Camus pulled no punches on this score: "Living the absurd . . . means a total lack of hope (which is not the same as despair), a permanent rejection (which is not the same as renunciation), and a conscious dissatisfaction (which is not the same as juvenile anxiety)."

Can we handle it? Or do we escape by saving our bodies and letting our soul and minds leap for us? Do we become among those who, as Benjamin Franklin suggested, die at 25 but aren't buried until they are 70?

Camus and Kierkegaard are called existentialists. When you see that term these days it is often moored alongside another: angst. To suffer public angst or ask deep questions without good answers is to be a bit quaint and out of touch — a Woody Allen in a world full of Bill and Hillary Clintons. In fact, even to admit such doubts is a sign of weakness that might cost you a another date, if not a promotion or an election.

We prefer something less difficult, such as the comfort of conformity, illusory perfection, and the presumption of immortality. We live in a society that expects machines, including the human one, to work without flaw, and when they don't, we feel confused and let down. Such expectations and the optimism that drives them have helped to give us great medical, scientific and technological advances, but they have also made us less wise and alive than we might otherwise be. And so popular literature overflows with prescriptions, reforms, recipes, repairs and remodeling. As a good American, I have contributed my share, but like other good Americans I have also left out something important: What to do when it doesn't work? When nothing works? When no one even seems to care whether it works. And if no one else cares, why should you? Why bother?

◆ ◆ ◆

The most common reaction to despair may be no more dramatic than a sense of boredom, of apathy, and indifference. In many ways, this is precisely the response our culture would prefer. It makes us ideal consumers of experience and excitement and assures that we won't interfere with the flow of goods and services by introducing novel notions of how society might be better rearranged.

Or one might take that leap of faith towards something that protects us from the unknown. "Life is at the start a chaos in which one is lost," wrote José Ortega y Gasset:

> The individual suspects this, but he is frightened at finding himself face to face with this terrible reality, and tries to cover it over with a curtain of fantasy, where everything is clear. It does not worry him that his "ideas" are not true, he uses them as trenches for the defense of his existence, as scarecrows to frighten away reality.

And here lies the paradox of therapy or, as Ernest Becker calls it, psychological rebirth:

> If you get rid of the four-layered neurotic shield, the armor that covers the characterlogical lie about life, how can you talk about "enjoying" this Pyrrhic victory? The person gives up something restricting and illusory, it is true, but only to come face to face with something even more awful: genuine despair. Full humanness means full fear and trembling, at least some of the waking day. When you get a person to emerge into life, away from his dependencies, his automatic safety in the cloak of someone else's power, what joy can you promise him with the burden of his aloneness?

You don't have to be a psychiatrist to confront this anomaly. I have spent my journalistic life attempting to tell people things that will help them understand what is really happening around them. Yet the closer I have come to succeeding, the more resistance I have found. For some, even asking hard questions is a suspect activity. And why not? After all, I am stealing their scarecrows.

Fortunately, not everybody thinks so. My last book was about politics. After it was published, however, something unexpected happened. I found people writing and talking to me not so much about the ideas in the book — agreeing with this or castigating that — but about its hope, about the possibility that one could still change things for the better. These people hadn't been ready for politics because they simply didn't believe it would work.

Here's part of one letter from a recent college graduate who had read a chapter that was excerpted in *Utne Reader*:

> I am just out of college here in central Illinois and, while I hang out with a varied and intelligent group of friends, I am often

disturbed by our collective sense of boredom — or even apathy
— towards many of the very aspects of society we seem to rail
against continually. I gave your article to some of these friends
of mine and everyone agreed that we had been going about our
business all wrong. The only effective and lasting way to tackle
the tough, entrenched problems America presents is in a positive, almost cheerful mood; taking the negative all the time
only drags the protester down, and usually nothing will get
done.

Here's another:

> Funny thing, I've gone through most of my life assuming things
> will just take care of themselves and in any case how could one
> person make any kind of a difference anyway?. . . . I was driving
> to work and it occurred to me that despite the huge machine we
> all rather dumbly assume is taking care of everything, it really
> takes just a handful of people to make things right. And then
> your [radio] interview came on . . . The point you were making
> about human beings being the ones to make change — the first
> step of which is to care — really struck home since that realiza-
> tion had just hit me.

Another woman wrote me to say that the book had caused her to look anew
at her political involvement which, she said, had moved from apathetic to
pathetic.

But then a man in his 20s came up to me after a talk and said, "I arrived late
and I heard you mentioning choice, so I thought you must be talking about
abortion." He politely suggested that I be more cautious in using the term.

A word that was for me at the core of what it means to be alive and human
was for him simply the right to select a certain clinical procedure that would,
justifiably or not, actually prevent life. Between our differing views of that one
word's meaning lay several decades of freedom's decay, constriction of choice,
and evaporation of hope.

One side of the divide still hears echoes of Emerson: "The office of America
is to liberate, to abolish kingcraft, priestcraft, caste, monopoly, to pull down the
gallows, to burn up the bloody statute-book, to take in the immigrant, to open
the doors of the sea and the fields of the earth." From the other side comes the
voice of New York mayor Rudolph Giuliani: "Freedom is about authority.
Freedom is about the willingness of every single human being to cede to lawful
authority a great deal of discretion about what you do."

◆ ◆ ◆

It's not just the words that have changed. More than 30 years ago, a small group of Washington citizens set out to stop the construction of freeways that were headed through their homes, their neighborhoods, and one of the more attractive cities in America. My wife Kathy recalls going with me to a meeting of anti-freeway activists shortly after we married in 1966. Recently arrived from neat, orderly Wisconsin, she couldn't believe that this mere handful of people thought they actually were going to stop a freeway.

In fact, we weren't able to stop the one we discussed that night, but before the fight was over we had halted much of a road system that would have turned Washington into an East Coast Los Angeles.

We used every tool within our reach, including the law, music, and art. When city council meetings went awry, protesters would stand and sing, "Oh beautiful for spacious roads . . ," When the leader of the movement, commercial artist Sammie Abbott, discovered secret plans for a route through the middle of the black center city, he designed a oversized two-color poster that was plastered all over the affected neighborhood. Under a headline, "White Men's Road's Through Black Men's Homes," it clearly outlined in red every building that would be destroyed. Fearing a riot, the city backed off the freeway plan within a few weeks.

The homes in the path of the bulldozers belonged to both whites and blacks and the movement left a heritage of biracial politics that would soften some of the ethnic polarization of the city. Besides, when you held a rally and the main speakers were Grosvenor Chapman, president of the all-white Georgetown Citizens Association, and Reginald Booker, president of the militant Niggers Inc,, even the most dismissive politician had to take notice.

All that, though, was more than 30 years ago. Anne Heutte, one of those deeply involved, recalls that "the hard thing during the freeway fight was getting people to believe that it was really possible to change things." Today, what was once hard now seems impossible. A woman told me recently, "A lot of people are afraid of politics. A lot of people want to be told what to do." A Northwestern University student says of her classmates that they "seem to be scared of activism. It's better just to be quiet and go with the flow."

In 1999, the *Washington Post* published an article by the chair of Washington's Metropolitan Board of Trade. In it, John Schwieters argued that the region had made a terrible mistake by not becoming an East Coast Los Angeles. Schwieters' pitch: let's do now with freeways what those "special interests," i.e. ordinary citizens, prevented the city from doing in the 1960s. As I read the article, I began counting the troops currently on our side, our arsenal, our allies. Then I counted those who had moved out, sold out, died out, or burned out and tried to calculate the loss of spirit, hope and will. It was no illusion. Times had indeed changed.

Those around in periods when effort bore some rough correlation to result tend to overrate themselves and underrate their era in crediting their good fortune. Hard as we may have rowed, we were borne on favorable currents. And when we flagged, there were plenty of others who pulled our weight.

It's not like that now. Consider, for example, the problem of discovering unpleasant truths about our land. If a revolution takes place in the forest and no one reports it, does it make a sound? If the second coming occurred tomorrow, would the media cover it? There seems little doubt but that the civil rights, peace, and women's movement would have had far less salutary outcomes had they been forced to confront today's media and the skill with which it ignores what it doesn't like. Gone is the ground rule that once required social and political change to be covered — even if the publisher didn't approve of it. Gone is the notion that if you made news, they would come. In an age of corporatist journalism, in which Peter Jennings has become the professional colleague of Mickey Mouse and Donald Duck, it no longer matters. News is just another item in the multinational product line with little value outside of its contribution to market share and other corporate objectives.

Worse, it has become just about impossible to find anyone in power who is ashamed of this. In fact, it is just about impossible to find anyone in power who is ashamed of anything. For centuries, shame has been one of the most useful restraints on power. As Edmund Burke noted, "Whilst shame keeps its watch, virtue is not wholly extinguished in the heart." But one of the perks of contemporary power is to exist without shame.

Shame and its benign cousin, conscience, once served a less public but equally vital role. The belief that if one tried hard enough, you could draw clean water even from a seemingly dry well, kept many an activist striving beyond rational expectations.

But disillusionment set in. The civil rights activist John Lewis would later recall the attempt to unseat the all-white Mississippi delegation at the 1964 Democratic convention: "This was the turning point for the civil rights movement . . . Until then, despite every setback . . . the belief still prevailed that the system would work, the system would listen . . . We had played by the rules, done everything we were supposed to do, had arrived at the door-step and found the door slammed in our face." The writer Dorothy Allison has also spoken of betrayed optimism: "I had the idea that if you took America and shook it really hard it would do the right thing."

As such possibilities faded we eventually found ourselves in a time when the concept of *wrong* was just one more social construct to be argued about on a talk show, one more small obstacle people put in your way on your climb to the top. The effect on efforts for change was like trying to bake bread without yeast.

Moral sensibility became part of the folkways of the masses, exploitable for ratings, but not necessary or desirable for actual policy or for those who made it. Thus the time between when the prominent declared their shock at some behavior and when they declared that we "should move on and put this behind us" became ever shorter.

The reporter risking status by telling the truth, the government official risking employment by exposing the wrong, the civic leader refusing to go with the flow — these are all essential catalysts of change. A transformation in the order of things is not the product of immaculate conception; rather it is the end of something that starts with the willingness of just a few people to do something differently. There must then come a critical second wave of others stepping out of a character long enough to help it happen — such as the white Mississippian who spoke out for civil rights, the housewife who read Betty Friedan and became a feminist, the parents of a gay son angered by the prejudice surrounding him. But for such dynamics to work there must be space for non-conformity and places for new ideas and the chance to be left alone by those who would manipulate, commodify, or destroy our every thought.

To be sure, 30 years ago some of those seeking change — especially in the South — found themselves confronted with far more life-threatening dangers than does today's cultural rebel. But on average, activists today face a more hostile media, a more repressive government, a more passive and defeated potential constituency, and an extraordinary competition for people's time and interest. One reason for this is that the dogs and clubs of Bull Connor's cops have been replaced by far more subtle stratagems. For example, if you choose to challenge authority, you may be labeled delusional, dangerous, or both. In recent years, both state and media have taken to dubbing someone a "paranoid" or a "conspiracy theorist" simply for not accepting the conventional wisdom about a politician or issue.

Meanwhile the reliably non-rebellious are kept that way in part by a surge of messages implying that they are but a stone's throw from inadequacy or danger of some sort or other. For example, one of the greatest changes in the media in recent decades has been the spread of a nanny-like tone to its ministrations, exemplified by the mass hypochondria encouraged by disease-of-the week TV shows and sternly prescriptive health columns.

Usually missing from these accounts, however, is any suggestion that corporations, government, and the culture as a whole might play a role in our health. For example, breast cancer rates have increased throughout the world since 1930 about one to two percent a year. According to World Watch, when you take all the controllable and uncontrollable personal factors into account — from diet to age of first menstruation — only 20–30% of all breast cancers can be explained. Does the environment explain much of the rest? We don't know, but we do know politicians and the media aren't particularly interested in finding out. Nor was the national newsweekly that trumpeted a two-decade explosion in the rate of skin cancer without a single mention of environmental changes. And you certainly won't find a magazine in your doctor's office with the headline, "How Government Reform Can Reduce Breast Cancer Six Ways."

Similarly, economics can affect your health in ways ranging from your sense of well-being to not being able to afford a doctor, but you will never see an obituary that says, "Jones had been in poor wealth for many years." Culture also plays its part. For example, 50% more French men possess two of the four major heart attack risk factors than do American men, but French men are one-third less likely to die of the disease than are US males. On the other hand, the supposedly nonchalant Frenchman is 50% more likely to kill himself than is his American counterpart, nearly half again as likely to take a tranquilizer and 13 times more likely to go to a doctor because of depression.

Yet despite the importance of such external factors as economics, culture, and the environment, the overwhelming message of contemporary America is that you bear full responsibility for your own health. Our personal duties are awesome enough without adding to our lives blame for whatever physical, cultural, political, or psychological poisons are also about.

This is no less true of one's state of mind. To view our times as decadent and dangerous, to mistrust the government, to imagine that those in power as not concerned with our best interests is not paranoid but perceptive; to be depressed, angry or confused about such things is not delusional but a sign of consciousness. Yet our culture suggests otherwise.

But if all this is true, then why not despair? The simple answer is this: despair is the suicide of imagination. Whatever reality presses upon us, there still remains the possibility of imagining something better, and in this dream remains the frontier of our humanity and its possibilities. To despair is to voluntarily close a door that has not yet shut. The task is to bear knowledge without it destroying ourselves, to challenge the wrong without ending up on its casualty list. "You don't have to change the world," the writer Colman McCarthy has argued. "Just keep the world from changing you."

◆ ◆ ◆

Oddly, those who instinctively understand this best are often those who seem to have the least reason to do so — survivors of abuse, oppression, and isolation who somehow discover not so much how to beat the odds, but how to wriggle around them. They have, without formal instruction, learned two of the most fundamental lessons of psychiatry and philosophy:

> You are not responsible for that into which you were born.
> You are responsible for doing something about it.

These individuals move through life like a skilled mariner in a storm rather than as a victim at a sacrifice. Relatively unburdened by pointless and debilitating guilt about the past, uninterested in the endless regurgitation of the unalterable, they free themselves to concentrate upon the present and the future. They face the gale as a sturdy combatant rather than as cowering supplicant.

Judith Herman, a specialist in psychological trauma, says the most important principles of recovery for abused persons are "restoring power, choice, and control" and helping the abused reconnect with people who are important to them. In short: choice and community. Survivors understand this implicitly even if they can't or don't express it.

My friend Steven Wolin is a psychiatrist who has been particularly interested in children of alcoholics. Wolin described his training:

> In my psychiatric residency that followed medical school, I glibly applied the terminology of physical disease to the 'disorders' of behavior and the mind. Eventually, I became so immersed in pathology that I no longer even used the word *healthy*. Instead, I conceived of health as the absence of illness and referred to people who were well as "asymptomatic," "nonclinical," unhospitalized," or "have no severe disturbance." In retrospect, the worst offender was the term "unidentified," as if the only way I could know a person was by his or her sickness. The peculiar vocabulary that my colleagues and I used to describe our patients reflected our meager regard for the forces that keep people healthy. . . .

Wolin would come to call this the "damage model," in which "pathologies are layered on pathologies, and eventually the survivor is no better off than his or her troubled parents."

But slowly, both in his research and therapy, he found what the profession calls "clinical failures," which is to say that the damage model didn't hold up. Not only did Wolin discover that the transmission of addictive drinking from parent to child was not as predictable as he had expected, not only did some of the children lead surprisingly satisfying lives, but the prescribed therapeutic techniques did not always work as well as they might. Among the reasons:

+ There was too much focus on the past and not enough on how to build a future.
+ Instead of being energized, some survivors fell into what Wolin calls the "victim's trap."
+ The model overemphasized pain at the expense of possibility, causing some survivors, who had left the past behind, to begin feeling like walking time bombs trapped by the inference that family problems inevitably repeat themselves from generation to generation.

Some of Wolin's patients had done extremely well on their own. Among their techniques: not dwelling on the past, not blaming their parents, and not becoming victims. They discovered and built on their own strengths, deliberately improved upon their parents' lifestyles, consciously married into strong families, and replaced memories of bad family gatherings with satisfying rituals of their own.

Out of this tough and honest reevaluation of his own work, Wolin and his wife (a developmental psychologist) came up with what they called the "challenge model" in which the experience of damage is balanced by conscious and unconscious resiliencies, in which trouble is not denied but neither is it allowed to rule.

In *The Resilient Self,* Steven and Sybil Wolin list ways in which survivors reframe personal stories in order to rise above the troubles of their past: insight, independence, relationships, initiative, humor, creativity, and morality. Survivors often strike out on their own, find other adults to help them when their own family fails them, and reject their parents' image of themselves.

The book is not only a personal guide for those who are or would be survivors. It is, whether intended or not, also a political guide. After all, our country and culture often stand *in locus parentis* and many of the pathologies we associate with families are mirrored and magnified in the larger society. Yet when we seek political therapy we repeatedly run up against a damage model enticing or forcing whole communities or groups into victimhood and leading them towards blame or surrender rather than resilience.

If insight, independence, relationships, initiative, humor, creativity, and morality form sturdy support for personal resilience, might they not also serve us collectively as the abused offspring of a culture that is chronically drunk on its own power and conceits?

◆ ◆ ◆

Not far away from the Wolins' Washington office is a community centered around U Street, now known as Shaw, where for decades just such a collective form of survival thrived. It has been a particular interest of my historian wife, Kathryn Schneider Smith. In the wake of the Civil War, this area North of Washington's downtown — originally occupied by both whites and blacks — experienced a building boom. With Jim Crow and the coming of the streetcar, whites moved beyond the center city and blacks increasingly found themselves isolated. Until the modern civil rights movement and desegregation, this African-American community was shut out without a vote, without economic power, without access, and without any real hope that any of this would change.

Its response was remarkable. For example, in 1895 there were only about 15 black businesses in the area. By 1920, with segregation in full fury, there were more than 300.

Every aspect of the community followed suit. Among the institutions created within these few square miles was a building and loan association, a savings bank, the only good hotel in the Washington where blacks could stay, the first full-service black YMCA in the country, the Howard Theatre (which opened 20 years before Harlem's Apollo converted to black performances), and two first-rate movie palaces.

There were the Odd Fellows, the True Reformers, and the Prince Hall Lodge. There were churches and religious organizations, a summer camp, a photography club that produced a number of professional photographers, settlement houses, and the Washington Urban League.

Denied access to white schools, the community created a self-sufficient educational system good enough to attract suburban African-Americans students as well as teachers from all over the country. And just to the North, Howard University became the intellectual center of black America. You might have run into Langston Hughes, Jean Toomey, or Duke Ellington, all of whom made the U Street area their home before moving to New York.

This was a proud community. "We had everything we needed," recalls one older resident. "And we felt good about it. Our churches, our schools, banks, department stores, food stores. And we did very well."

The community shared responsibility for its children. A typical story went like this: "There was no family my family didn't know or that didn't know me. I couldn't go three blocks without people knowing exactly where I had been and everything I did on the way. It wasn't just the schools. We learned from everyone. We learned as much from Aunt So-and-So down the street, who was not even related to us."

All this occurred while black Washingtonians were being subjected to extraordinary economic obstacles and being socially and politically ostracized. If there ever was a culture entitled to despair and apathy it was black America under segregation.

Yet not only did these African-Americans develop self-sufficiency, they did so without taking their eyes off the prize. Among the other people you might have found on U Street were Thurgood Marshall and Charles Houston, laying the groundwork for the modern civil rights movement.

Years later, while serving on a NAACP task force on police and justice, I would go to a large hall in the organization's headquarters — at the same U Street address that was on the 1940s flyers calling for civil rights protests. In that hall, except for the addition of a few plaques, nothing much has changed over the decades. We only needed two tables pushed together so there was plenty of room for the ghosts of those who once sat around such tables asking the same questions, seeking the same solutions, striving for some way for decency to get a foothold. Basic legal strategies for the civil rights movement were planned along this street. Did perhaps Thurgood Marshall or Clarence Mitchell once sit at one end of this hall and also wonder what to do next? Just the question lent courage.

With the end of segregation, as free choice replaced a community of necessity, the area around U Street began to change. The black residents dispersed.

Eventually the street would become better known for its crime and drugs, and as the birthplace of the 1968 riots. The older residents would remember the former neighborhood with a mixture of pain and pride — not unlike the ambivalence found in veterans recalling a war. None would voluntarily return to either segregation or the battlefield but many would know that some of their own best moments of courage, skill, and heart had come when the times were at their worst. Some of the people in this community were only a couple of generations away from slavery, some had come from Washington's early free black community. But whatever their provenance, they had learned to overcome despair and become self-sufficient in fact and spirit even as they battled to end the injustices that required them to be so.

◆ ◆ ◆

One black woman with whom I worked closely, Josephine Butler, first went on a picket line in the 1930s. Only multiple heart attacks in the mid-1990s stopped her from doing so again. The last time I saw Jo Butler in the intensive care unit we discussed books. Though burdened with the cold, involuntary appendages of medical technology, Jo spoke with the same enthusiasm she applied to the latest political developments.

In fact, there was little — from earthworms to earth-shaking — that did not stir Jo's curiosity and, when required, her compassionate and effective concern. Though her heart might be filled with the overwhelming political and social problems of our time, her eye was always on the sparrow and she seldom wasted much time on sorrow.

I loved to run into Jo on the street — her bag overflowing with yet-to-be-distributed documents of truth and her hat bedizened with buttons — campaign ribbons from the endless battlefields where she had stood on the side of the fair, the decent, and the just. She carried the spirit of the city and the spirit of hope not as a possession or a totem, but as seeds to share with anyone who would stop and talk for a moment or two.

She had worked longer for, and lost more battles on behalf of, justice than anyone I ever met, yet I never saw her fearful, impatient or exhausted. She would, from time to time, show up on my block of Connecticut Avenue like some angel on a temporal inspection tour. We would talk, and laugh, and worry together and when we parted I would always feel more directed, more responsible for what was happening around me, but also happier and braver and more willing to try the difficult one more time. She lived that life so well described by the poet Samuel Hazo, filled with "hard questions and the nights to answer them, and grace of disappointment, and the right to seem the fool for justice."

POSSIBILITIES

Ways of Being

Rebellion

Witness

Others

Guerrilla Democracy

Hat Trick

WAYS OF BEING

We'll return to our present circumstances in a moment. But first, let's go to a time and place so distant that no one knows when or where it was, a time and place whose importance is as infinite as its obscurity.

The moment we are seeking is the one during which a single individual, or a small group of individuals, did something so unusual that it helped free their ilk forever from the shackles of the environment and genetics — grabbing destiny from the tree of nature and making it human.

According to conventional theory it may have happened as long as 400,000 years ago in a place still — and probably forever — uncertain. This extraordinary coup against the unknown was the simple taming of fire, the stealing of light and heat from a cryptic, tyrannical universe, transforming it into a matter of personal choice. No subsequent human event would be more important yet the names and descriptions of the suspects are still unknown.

Since we have been told so little, however, we are free to imagine. It might even help in what follows if we do. Give him, her, or them a name, a height and weight, a face, a way of moving, a home, a time of day. A high bluff? A small cave? Under a lonely tree in the savanna?

And then the act itself. A flame accidentally born from a struck rock's spark, the memory of how this accident happened never to be forgotten? Or the gift of lightning preserved forever? Then the next steps: The cooking. The carrying of the flame to camps which had never seen such a thing. The gathering of others around the incredible creation and the sharing of the mystery.

On the first day of my freshman anthropology class, the professor drew an invisible evolutionary time line on the wall of the lecture hall. As we twisted in our seats the earth's eras, periods, and epochs of musical name and mystical significance boldly circumscribed the room. Finally we came back to where the professor stood and when there was nearly no place further to go, he announced that this was the beginnings of us. We were only inches from the fire maker.

I became an anthropology major and my relationship with the fire maker, and with the creator of the stone ax, the inventor of the spear thrower, and the first potter, would never cease to be both humbling and glorious. Humbling because our true evolutionary insignificance daily mocks our pretensions. Yet also glorious because without the endless random reiteration of individual creation, choice, and imagination, we might be shivering in the dark instead of reading a book with our feet up and wondering whether there's another beer in the fridge. We are nothing and everything, inexplicably and inseparably bundled together.

Though not inclined to scrounge for shards or delineate kinship systems for a living, I nonetheless enjoyed the anthropologists and their teachings. I even began to play anthropologist among the anthropologists, noticing, among other things, that they tended to be somewhat out of sync with their own culture. These teachers did not talk or act like other scholars. I suspected that many shared with me the fantasy that in our studies we might uncover a society whose idiosyncrasies matched our own. Even the musty old museum in which they carried out their business sat, like an Amazonian tribe, distinctly away from the main campus.

Elsewhere at the university, students were being taught about great men and great revolutions and great thoughts, receiving in Talmudic fashion the master truths of the American establishment — those approved categories into which all of life's experiences could be safely stuffed along with the proper meanings and words with which they could be explained.

Once inside the anthropology museum, however, this greatness became but a tiny part of the total greatness of the human world; the master truths of America began to shrivel and not seem that great after all.

I didn't know it then, but I had joined not so much a discipline as a rebellion. Under the guise of studying the often rigid rules, customs, and traditions of different human communities, anthropology was actually opening a benign Pandora's box of choice, laying before the world its own wondrous variety, opportunity, and concomitant pain and joy.

It was not a popular rebellion. Only one or two of my courses had more than 20 students. Years later, academics and media would discover something they called multiculturalism or diversity. They would speak of it in ponderous tones and as their discovery, and they would describe it as a problem and demand that we do something about it. Too few would notice that what we were talking about as a problem was really a gift and an opportunity and a potential source of our own happiness and freedom.

◆ ◆ ◆

For nearly all of human history, the dilemmas that cause people to write books like this, visit psychiatrists, or take philosophy courses in college, were largely moot. In the West, the idea that humans could have significant control over the definition of their own morality gained popularity only a few centuries ago, spurred by the spread of the Enlightenment and other subversive ideas. With it, humans were no longer depraved, unworthy applicants for post-mortal celestial immigration. With it, they could have virtue, knowledge, power, and possibility, all within their present existence. And with it came choices and the responsibility to make them.

Similarly, those things some call "issues," such as personal freedom, individual character, and dreams of success or power have not always been problems for most. Throughout most human time, the individual has either been assigned a role or allowed to choose from a narrow menu of choices.

Yet even within such constraints, the range of culturally defined behavior has been remarkable. Consider, for example, the Ojibwa of Canada, described by Brian Morris in *Anthropology of the Self.* These Indians, a group of nomadic hunters and fishers,

> do not make any categorical or sharply defined differentiation between myth and reality, or between dreaming and the waking state; neither can any hard or fast line be drawn between humans and animals. . . . A bear is an animal which unlike humans hibernates during the winter, but in specific circumstances it may be interpreted as a human sorcerer. . . . The four winds are thought of not only as animate by the Ojibwa, but are categorized as persons.

Not only may a culture define the four winds as persons under certain circumstances, it may also define a slave or someone from another tribe as not a person at all. Nonetheless the slave or the outsider really exist so at some level are treated as a person anyway. Hence people in such societies may trade goods with the stranger or attempt to convert the slave to Christianity even though they are not considered human. Or the society may try to quantify such anomalies as Americans did when they declared a black legally equal to three-fifths of a white person. Or it may create a hierarchy as Aristotle did when he confidently declared that "the deliberative faculty in the soul is not present at all in a slave: in a female is present but ineffective, in a child present but undeveloped." Or it may declare that "all men are created equal" but really mean only white male property owners. Or it may fight a revolution for liberty but leave women as chattel. Or the culture can painfully change such values over two centuries and still have to go repeatedly to court to fight over what was really meant by the change.

Cultural vainglory doesn't help us wade through this. For example, in this book there are a number of quotes from the past that use the word *man* or *men* where today we would use a word such as *people*. In some cases this is merely an archaic convention, in others it reflects the substantial cultural blinders of the writers and their times. We tend to be smug and critical about such matters but consider this: the median age of Americans in 1830 was 16. Teenagers ran businesses, farmed, and captained ships instead of being regarded as problem dependents or potential criminals and mass killers. Similarly, many cultures have treated older people with far greater respect and honor than does our supposedly enlightened country. Just as racial segregation seemed normal to Southern whites before the civil rights movement, so today our prejudices against the young and the old are sufficiently ingrained that we don't even talk much about them.

In such ways do we suffer from a little noted form of prejudice one might call aerobicism, which is to say the assumption that the living are morally superior to the dead. As the historian Barbara Tuchman has noted, "To understand the choices open to people of another time, one must limit oneself to what they knew; see the past in its own clothes, as it were, not in ours."

◆ ◆ ◆

Here is how anthropologist Morris describes his own Western culture:

> It is individualistic, and has a relatively inflated concern with the self which in extremes gives rise to anxiety, to a sense that there is a loss of meaning in contemporary life, to a state of narcissism, and to an emphasis in popular psychology on 'self actualization.'

Bad as this sounds, though, you will probably get along better in New York or Chicago with a loss of meaning, state of narcissism, or overflowing self-actualization than if you try to escape your angst by acting like the Ojibwa. In the Big Apple, to lack a sharply defined differentiation between myth and reality, between dreaming and the waking state; or between humans and animals, risks not only ridicule but actual legal sanctions. Our culture claims to celebrate the power of the individual, but the restraints on that individualism are substantial and we, like peoples everywhere, go about our daily business regarding them as largely normal.

If you try to break this pattern — as the deconstructionists of postmodernism have — you may find yourself in the awkward position of understanding just how silly society's existing rules are yet being unable to replace them with anything better because your own rules declare this to be impossible. The result of shattering truths, meta-narratives, and communal myths can be a form of anarchy in which only power and propaganda rule, and the 800-pound relativist gets to do just what it wants.

In fact, while the range of choices, values, and constraints among cultures is stunning in its variety, it is impossible to find a functioning society in which choices have not been made. Similarly, though individuals may reject society and even design their own micro-cultures, they are no less dependent on their decisions, whether conscious or not. To not make them is to drift aimlessly and lifelessly, pushed this way or that by others quite anxious and ready to make choices for you.

Unfortunately, we receive little instruction in how to deal with this. Anthropologists, other academics, and journalists prefer to aggregate individual variety into something both grander and simpler, politely known as a culture, paradigm, ideology, or trend, or (if you don't care for the resulting generalizations) a stereotype. Thus we have little sense of what it is like to be a punk Buddhist, a Hindu convert to Unitarianism or a follower of both Confucianism and the Dallas Cowboys. The mere number of cultural traits and values available for adoption in a world in which the grandchildren of Margaret Mead's anthropological subjects watch MTV has engorged us with possibilities.

The embedded individual

For most of human existence, though, the individual was thoroughly embedded in one culture, sometimes so deeply that what we think of as individualism seems to disappear. For example, in India, writes Agehananda Bharati,

> When any of the Hindu traditions speak about what might be like the individual, like an empirical self, it is not to analyze it but to denigrate it . . . The self as the basis of such important human achievements as scholarship, artistic skill, technological invention, etc., is totally ignored in the Indian philosophical texts.

For the traditional Hindu, family and caste leave little room for individualism and personal autonomy. Does this mean there is no Indian dissent? Gandhi and his followers certainly proved otherwise, as does the Indian cab driver grilling you about job opportunities in your profession or the Indian doctor feeling your pulse in the Kansan hospital. Every immigrant is another saga of cultural insurrection, a tribute to the enduring human capacity for individual choice. Even for Indians in their own country, writes Morris, "achieving a degree of personal autonomy is an important theme of adult life and this is often associated with rebellions against the caste hierarchies."

Such a highly sociocentric approach to life is far from unique, but can occur in many ways. Among the Gahuku-Gama of New Guinea, for example, there is no clear distinction between individuals and their cultural status. Kenneth Read observed that for the Gahuku-Gama, people are "not conceived to be equals in a moral sense; their value does not reside in themselves as individuals or persons; it is dependent on the position they occupy within a system of inter-personal and inter-group relationships."

Which, in turn, is not that far from a culture described by C. Wright Mills:

> If we took the one hundred most powerful men in America, the one hundred wealthiest, and the one hundred most cele-brated away from the institutional positions they now occupy, away from their resources of men and women and money, away from the media of mass communication . . . then they would

be powerless and poor and uncelebrated. For power is not of a man. Wealth does not center in the person of the wealthy. Celebrity is not inherent in any personality. To be celebrated, to be wealthy, to have power, requires access to major institutions, for the institutional positions men occupy determine in large part their chances to have and to hold these valued experiences.

On the other hand, if you were a Balinese Hindu, you would find yourself in a *banjar*, a community association around which much of your life would revolve.

Bali's topography, with its rugged slopes and gorges, has encouraged the self-sufficiency of communities, producing, among other things, the *subak*, a cooperative that plans rice irrigation projects, builds and repairs aqueducts and dikes. As with the *banjar*, membership and fees in the subak are mandatory. Fail to show for a meeting of either one and you will be assessed a fine.

This is not some regulatory scheme imposed by the state, but part of a cultural tradition that goes back at least 11 centuries. *Banjar* members can be called to do manual labor for the village, attend and help to organize weddings and funerals, work in a restaurant as a part of a festival, help maintain the temple, or play in the village orchestra. Said one *banjar* member quoted by Fred B. Eisenman Jr. in *Bali: Sekala and Niskala*:

> In a small town, one's absence is quickly noticed. And next time you require help from others, it may not be forthcoming. There are usually two or three times as many people in a work group as are required for the work to be done. One is not really needed. No matter. One must be seen participating. Good reputations are important when people are shoulder to shoulder.

An American present at a wedding noted a group of attendees not wearing traditional Balinese dress. They were, it was explained, from the local bank, which had closed for the day to fulfill its workers' responsibilities to the *banjar*. In fact, some tourist hotels hire Javanese rather than Balinese workers because the former's community duties are not so time-consuming.

◆ ◆ ◆

In African culture, the individual may be subordinated to outside forces in complex relationships where, reports one scholar, "subject and object are not longer distinguishable." In other words, the force may not only be with you, but in you. One anthropologist describes the Bantu as never being isolated individuals but always part of a chain of vital forces.

Some of this can get pretty heavy, even annoying. Morris notes that if you were one of the Tallensi of Northern Ghana your primary obligation would be to your ancestors who, if unhappy with your conduct, might spread trouble in your path or even kill you. On the other hand, the Ashanti of Ghana, while sociocentric and sharing their souls with spirits, have a more benign, almost Quaker-like, approach. They possess okra, described by one anthropologist as "the small bit of the creator who lives in every body" — much as the Friends believe that there is something of God in every person.

Of such African cultures, John Mbiti has written:

> Whatever happens to the individual happens to the whole group, and whatever happens to the whole group happens to the individual. The individual can only say: "I am, because we are, and since we are, therefore I am."

Such a view is not unknown in Western thought, witness Hillel's oft-quoted questions:

> If I am not for myself, who is for me?
> But if I am only for myself, what am I?

Another anthropologist has described the African approach as more as a matter of dual responsibility to oneself and to the group. Such a dualism can be manifested in a number of ways including a modesty and lack of self-assertion that Americans might find odd. Robert Le Vine writes that among the Gussi of Western Kenya, for example, it is "conventional for individuals to conceal from others any information about one's advantages, good fortune or positive events that would portray the self in favorable terms. . . . Our [i.e., American middle class] 'healthy self-esteem' is conceit and selfishness by their standards."

Similarly, Matt Ridley describes a highland people in central New Guinea who have taken up football but, "finding it a little too much for the blood pressure to lose a game, they have adjusted the rules. The game simply continues until each side has scored a certain number of goals. A good time is had by all, but there is no loser and every goal scorer can count themselves a winner."

And here is Ruth Benedict writing of the Zuni of the Southwest:

> The ideal man in Zuni is a person of dignity and affability who has never tried to lead, and who has never called forth comment from his neighbors. Any conflict, even though all right is on his side, is held against him. Even in contests of skill like their foot races, if a man wins habitually he is debarred from running. They are interested in a game that a number can play with even

chances, and an outstanding runner spoils the game: they will have none of him.

The ideal Zuni described by Benedict avoids office. He may have it thrust upon him, but he does not seek it. When the kiva offices must be filled, the hatchway of the kiva is fastened and all the men are imprisoned until someone's excuses have been battered down. The folk tales describe good men and their unwillingness to take office — though in the end they always assume it, much as Benjamin Franklin professed that he had never sought a public office — nor refused one.

Beyond cultural constraints, there's also the environment to consider. Taoists are subordinated not to parents, caste, the past, or mysterious forces, but to nature, as suggested by a Taoist song:

> As the sun rises I get up
> As the sun sets I go to rest
> I dig a well for my drink
> I till the field for my food.
> What has the power of the emperor to do with me?

Similar ecocentrism can be found among the Yupiaq, of whom Angayuqaq Oscar Kawagley of the University of Alaska has written

> For the Yupiaq people, culture, knowing, and living are intricately interrelated. Living in a harsh environment requires a vast array of precise empirical knowledge to survive the many risks due to conditions such as unpredictable weather and marginal food availability. To avoid starvation they must employ a variety of survival strategies, including appropriate storage of foodstuffs that they can fall back on during the time of need. Their food gathering and storage must be efficient as well as effective. . . . To help them achieve this balance, they have developed an outlook of nature as metaphysic.
>
> Not only are humans endowed with consciousness, but so are all things of the environment. The Yupiaq people live in an aware world. Wherever they go they are amongst spirits of their ancestors, as well as those of the animals, plants, hills, winds, lakes and rivers. Their sense of sacredness is of a practical nature, not given to abstract deities and theological rationalization. . . . Because nature is their metaphysic, Yupiaq people are concerned with maintaining harmony in their own environment.

◆ ◆ ◆

Yet another approach is that of a Buddhist, who, writes Walpola Rabula, gets along without a soul or a god, and seeks to transcend the absurdity of the universe and the suffering that goes with it. Morris sees Buddhism as an extreme form of individualism "for there is no recourse to a deity or savior, no prayer or sacrament, no religious grace, and not even an enduring soul." Each individual carries personal responsibility for things thought, done, and spoken. The Buddha, it has been said, provides the raft of enlightenment from which to depart suffering and impermanence in order to get to the other shore of bliss and safety.

But this is an unusual form of individualism because, as Rabula points out, "according to the teaching of the Buddha, the idea of self is an imaginary, false belief which has no corresponding reality, and it produces harmful thoughts of 'me' and 'mine,' selfish desire, craving, attachment, hatred, ill-will, conceit, pride, egoism, and other defilements, impurities and problems."

Breaking free

It is tempting in a time when our society seems so destructive of its own kind and when we have such easy access to alternatives to treat culture as just another commodity.

The Buddist nun Pema Chodron warns against this. In *The Wisdom of No Escape*, she recalls being invited to speak at a weekend program that was a kind of "New Age spiritual shopping mart . . . There was this big poster, like a school bulletin board, that said Basic Goodness, Room 606; Rolfing, Room 609; Astral Travel, Room 666; and so forth."

She cites one of her teachers as having said that shopping is about trying to find security, always trying to feel good about yourself. Instead, "when one sticks to one boat, whatever that boat may be, then one actually begins the warrior's journey." The danger in the alternative is that "the minute you really begin to hurt, you'll just leave or you'll look for something else." We stop rowing and seek yet another craft to carry us onward.

As we become more aware of our options — or more sophisticated, as we like to call it — the choices we have already made, or have been made for us, may lose their allure and we can find ourselves wandering in a cultural void somewhere between the Trobriand Islands and Trenton.

A detachment from one's indigenous culture can set in, a trait observable in diplomats, military personnel, international business executives, and anthropologists. It is not that they are without a culture: rather, theirs becomes a culture that lacks place. This can have some odd results, such as the anthropologist's high school daughter who begged that the family at least stay in the US her senior year so she would have a room to remember as "home" when she went to college.

One of the things driving such restlessness is an assumption that our own culture must inevitably be locked in combat with our own nature. In drawing this conclusion we may place inordinate emphasis on the faults of our parents, the sins of the marketplace, racism, and the "oppression of the system." This is not to say that these wrongs do not exist and need not be confronted, only that they hardly define the whole of our culture's influence on us. As Americans, for example, it tells nothing of values of pragmatism, fairness, reinvention, and freedom that have survived the worst years of our collective experience. Ruth Benedict put it like this:

> In reality, society and the individual are not antagonists. His culture provides the raw material of which the individual makes his life. If it is meager, the individual suffers; if it is rich, the individual has the chance to rise to his opportunity. Every private interest of every man and woman is served by the enrichment of the traditional stores of his civilization. The richest musical sensitivity can operate only within the equipment and standards of its tradition. It will add, perhaps importantly, to that tradition. But its achievement remains in proportion to the instruments and musical theory which the culture has provided. . . . No culture yet observed has been able to eradicate the differences in the temperaments of the persons who compose it.

Which doesn't mean cultures don't try. Writing more than 60 years ago, Benedict cited homosexuality as the kind of non-conformance to which cultures can react in different ways:

> The American Indians do not make Plato's high moral claims for homosexuality, but homosexuals are often regarded as exceptionally able. [When] the homosexual response is regarded as a perversion, however, the invert is immediately exposed to all the conflicts to which aberrants are always exposed. His guilt, his sense of inadequacy, his failures, are consequences of the disrepute which social tradition visits upon him. . . .

And she concluded her discussion with words worth keeping handy in today's America: "Tradition is as neurotic as any patient; its overgrown fear of deviation from its fortuitous standards conforms to all the usual definitions of the psychopathic."

Killing culture

Far worse than cultural neurosis or nomadism, however, is the destruction of culture itself. There are still, for example, about 6,700 languages in the world but only about 200 of these are official tongues of a country or carry with them enough cultural force to ensure their survival. According to Guy Gugliotta in the *Washington Post*, at least one language disappears every two weeks and many linguists believe that at least 3,000 will vanish over the next 100 years. Reports Gugliotta: "In Australia, linguists estimate that 90 percent of what used to be 250 languages are moribund. In Alaska, Siberia and the rest of the polar North, 56 of 72 languages are disappearing. In the Amazon jungle, 82 of 100 to 150 languages appear doomed."

The death of these languages is not just of scholarly interest. Each lost tongue is a form of genocide by amnesia and a contraction of human possibility. As Mitchell Kraus, director of the Alasaka Native Language Center, puts it, "Every time we lose a language, we lose a whole way of thinking." And a whole different way of being human.

Languages can also disintegrate internally. David Orr, writing in *Utne Reader*, reported that "in the past 50 years, by one reckoning, the working vocabulary of the average 14-year-old had declined from 25,000 words to 10,000. This is a decline not merely in words, but also in the capacity to think. We are losing the capacity to say what we mean, and ultimately to think about what we mean, about the things that matter most."

Part of this is the inevitable result of improved communications, creating a paradigm-rattling assault on both culture and individuality — what the semiotician Marshall Blonsky calls the "semiosphere, a dense atmosphere of signs triumphantly permeating all social, political, and imaginative life and, arguably, constituting our desiring selves as such."

Even our own words become just another product foisted upon us from the outside; we learn to adapt and restrict our language to that of the commercial and technocratic systems that control so much of our lives. And as our words contract, so does our world.

This semiosphere — bombarding us with the UV rays of advertising, propaganda, or just interminable sounds and sights devoid of meaning — is controlled in large part by multinational corporations whose intentions include the destruction of both culture and individuality. Their goal, well described by the French writer Jacques Attali, is an "ideologically homogenous market where life will be organized around common consumer desires."

This new world is unlike any in human history, a world in which the destruction of cultural and individual variety — from the nation state to the remnants of the Objibwa — is high on the agenda of the earth's political and business leaders; the very heart of our human nature being to them not a reason for existence but just another obstacle in their path to power.

Recovering culture

One response to society's assault of human variation is the creation of an "identity," around which the icons, values, and artifacts of a culture are consciously built. Identity cultures — such as the black, lesbian or disabled "community" — are intentionally designed to end discrimination but perhaps also are unconsciously part of a broader reaction to the threat against culture itself. Many may feel the need for an identity not merely because of prejudice against their own ethnicity, but against the biggest race of all, the human one.

The obvious advantage of identity culture is the protection of a group. The less obvious disadvantage is that over-emphasis on one's status, sex, or ethnicity can be just as much an obstacle to individualism as, say, loyalty to the corporate culture. It converts context into classification. When someone stands up in a meeting and says, "Speaking as a gay Jew. . ." they are defining themselves as far less than they really are.

This is a point that *Star Trek*'s Captain Jean-Luc Picard understood. Lt. Commander Data, the android officer aboard the starship Enterprise, had a vision of his creator, Doctor Soong. He tries to get Captain Picard to help him interpret the vision:

> DATA: I have analyzed over four thousand different religious and philosophical systems as well as over two hundred psychological schools of thought in an effort to understand what happened.
>
> PICARD: And what have you found?
>
> DATA: I've been unable to find a single interpretation of the images I saw during the time I was shut down. The hammer, for instance, has several meanings. The Klingon culture views the hammer as a symbol of power, however, the Tapo tribe of Nagor sees it as an icon of hearth and home. The Ferengii view it as a sign of sexual prowess.
>
> PICARD: I'm curious, Mr. Data. Why are you looking at all these other cultures?
>
> DATA: The interpretation of visions and other metaphysical experiences are almost always culturally derived and I have no culture of my own.
>
> PICARD: Yes, you do. You're a culture of one. Which is no less valid than a culture of one billion. Perhaps the key to understanding your experience is to stop looking into other sources for meaning. When we look at Michelangelo's David or Seme's Tomb we don't ask what does this mean to other people. The real question is what does it mean to us.

Anthropologist Steve Mizrach, explained Picard's comments this way:

Symbols, icons, signs, and all the other things that go to make
up a culture come to have meaning to an individual because of
past life experiences and everything is interpreted through
filters. But what are some of these filters, these past life experiences, through which everything is interpreted? The filters
through which everything experienced is interpreted can be
thought of as the individual's culture.

◆ ◆ ◆

Of course, we don't have to do it all alone. One of the most fascinating and
unusual examinations of how culture can be redefined is contained in a strange
book, *T.A.Z. The Temporary Autonomous Zone, Ontological Anarchy, Poetic
Terrorism*, by Hakim Bey. Bey argues that the world fundamentally changed
with what he calls the "closure of the map" — the end of terrestrial discovery:

> Because the map is an abstraction it cannot cover earth with 1:1
> accuracy. Within the fractal complexities of actual geography
> the map can see only dimensional grids. Hidden enfolded
> immensities escape the measuring rod.

For example, there is the map one might draw of the Internet, whose nomads
may never leave their office or room. They are like Thoreau who said he had
"traveled much — in Concord." Says Bey:

> Lay down a map of the land; over that set a map of political
> change; over that a map of the Net, especially the counter-Net
> with its emphasis on clandestine information-flow and logistics
> — and finally, over all, the 1:1 map of the creative imagination,
> aesthetics, values. The resultant grid comes to life, animated by
> unexpected eddies and surges of energy, coagulations of light,
> secret tunnels, surprises.

Bey's temporary autonomous zones are uncertain and undulating communities of the rootless and the alienated:

> The TAZ is like an uprising which does not engage directly with
> the state, a guerrilla operation which liberates an area (of land,
> of time, of imagination) and then dissolves itself to re-form else-
> where/elsewhen, before the state can crush it. Because the state
> is concerned primarily with simulation rather than substance,
> the TAZ can "occupy" these areas clandestinely and carry on its
> festal purposes for quite a while in relative peace. Perhaps

certain small TAZs have lasted whole lifetimes because they went unnoticed — like hillbilly enclaves — because they never intersected with the spectacle, never appeared outside that real life which is invisible to the agents of simulation.

An example is the pirate utopia:

> The sea-rovers and corsairs of the 18th century created an "information network" that spanned the globe: primitive and devoted primarily to grim business; the net nevertheless functioned admirably. Scattered throughout the net were islands, remote hideouts where ships could be watered and provisioned, booty traded for luxuries and necessities. Some of these islands supported "intentional communities," whole mini-societies living consciously outside the law and determined to keep it up, even if only for a short but merry life . . . Fleeing from hideous "benefits" of imperialism such as slavery, serfdom, racism and intolerance, from the tortures of impressment and the living death of the plantations, the buccaneers adopted Indian ways, intermarried with Caribs, accepted blacks and Spaniards as equals, rejected all nationality, elected their captains democratically, and reverted to the "state of nature." Having declared themselves "at war with all the world," they sailed forth to plunder under mutual contracts called "Articles" which were so egalitarian that every member received a full share and the captain usually only 1¼ or 1½ shares . . .

The business of building cultures within, beyond, and without existing ones is fraught with possibility, disappointment and danger. It has led to the Montana Militia, secret cop fraternities, intentional communities, even more intentional dictatorships, religious orders, feminist affinity groups, the Crips, the civil rights movement, Alcoholics Anonymous, and Woodstock.

The 1960s, in many ways, was a huge temporary autonomous zone, as are many periods of great social and political change. The fragility of such chronological cultures hurtling through a small window of opportunity is often missed by their members. In the 1960s, Bobby Seale presciently warned, "seize the time," but for many, it seemed no more likely that the Age of Aquarius would disintegrate than it might have seemed possible to post-Civil War radical Republicans that their work of reconstruction would be undone barely a dozen years after it started.

Still, history favors eruptions more than steady processions, and these uprisings, brief as they may be, are the major seasons of social and political change. For example, though few remember the Dutch Provos of the 1960s, they laid the foundation for the Green Party and for the anti-drug prohibition and shorter-workweek movements. They offer a good example of how even during the most recalcitrant eras, there are tools of change available if individuals use their imaginations without awaiting the grace of power and if they can, as Carlos Baker said of Ralph Waldo Emerson, help create the culture that will nurture them.

Writing of the Provos in *High Times* magazine, Teun Voeten said, "They were the first to combine non-violence and absurd humor to create social change." Their provenance could not have been more puerile: disaffected Dutch teens known as Nozems: "Part mods, part '50s juvenile delinquents, they spent most of their time cruising the streets on mopeds, bored stiff and not knowing what to do. Their favorite past-time? Raising trouble and provoking the police."

A timid and introverted philosophy student, Roel Van Duyn, saw their political potential, proclaiming in 1965, "It is our task to turn their aggression into revolutionary consciousness." Meanwhile a former window cleaner and "original clown prince of popular culture," Robert Jasper Grootveld, was already laying some of the foundation:

> Grootveld staged Saturday night happenings, wearing strange clothes and performing to growing crowds of Nozems, intellectuals, curious bypassers, and police. Writer Harry Mulisch described it this way: "While their parents, sitting on their refrigerators and dishwashers, were watching with their left eye the TV, with their right eye the auto in front of the house, in one hand the kitchen mixer, in the other *De Telegraaf,* their kids went out Saturday night to the Spui Square . . . And when the clock struck twelve, the high priest appeared, all dressed up, from some alley and started to walk magic circles around the nicotinistic demon, while his disciples cheered. applauded and sang the Ugge Ugge song."

The Provos created various "White Plans," including the White Bike Plan which called for replacing cars in the inner city with white bicycles, to be provided by the government. The bikes would be left unlocked so anyone could use them. Among other White Plans:

- Anyone causing a fatal car accident should be forced to paint the outline of their victim's body on the pavement at the site of the accident. That way, no one could ignore the fatalities caused by automobiles
- The White Chimney Plan (put a heavy tax on polluters and paint their chimneys white)
- The White Kids Plan (free daycare centers)
- The White Housing Plan (stop real estate speculation)
- The White Wife Plan (free medical care for women) . . .

The Provos eventually became so influential that they could no longer pass as the consummate alienated. Voeten describes their end:

> The reason for Provo's demise, which was totally unexpected by outsiders, was its increasing acceptance by moderate elements, and growing turmoil within its ranks. As soon as Provo began participating in the city council elections, a transformation occurred. A Provo Politburo emerged, consisting of VIP Provos who began devoting most of themselves to political careers. Provos toured the country, giving lectures and interviews . . . The division between the street Provos and the reformist VIPs began growing wider. Some Provos returned to their studies,. others went hippie and withdrew from the movement . . . Provo held one last stunt. A white rumor was spread that American universities wanted to buy the Provo archives, documents that actually didn't exist. Amsterdam University, fearing that the sociological treasure might disappear overseas, quickly made an offer the Provos couldn't refuse. . . .

The Provos' politics revolved around symbolism that mocked, reversed and distorted the official symbols of the state. Their heirs include Abbie Hoffman, and the turn-of-the-century protesters against the IMF and World Bank.

◆ ◆ ◆

What does all this have to do with you and me? For one thing, it means that our own culture, for all its wonders and faults, represents but a tiny fraction of the choices humans have collectively made over time and space. These choices, distant as they may be, beckon us towards possibilities lying dormant within ourselves. They also mock the self-assurance with which we run our little corner of the world.

Secondly, the nature of culture is drastically changing from being something into which the individual is indoctrinated and absorbed, towards something the individual must preserve, restore or recreate in order to avoid the destruction of all culture save that of the corporate market and the political systems that support it.

Finally, the strategies by which this can be accomplished depend on no small part on the imagination, passion, obstinacy, and creativity of ordinary people who refuse their consumptive assignments in the global marketplace, who develop autonomous alternatives, and who laugh when they are supposed to be saluting. The business of constructing culture is no longer an inherited and precisely defined task but a radical act in defense of our individual and collective souls.

REBELLION

The words *revolution* and *rebellion* attract unjust opprobrium. After all, much of what we identify as peculiarly American is ours by grace of our predecessors' willingness to revolt in the most militant fashion, and their imperfect vision has been improved by a long series of rebellions ranging from the cerebral to the bloody. There is not an American alive who has not been made better by revolution and rebellion.

In fact, the terms sit close to what it means to human, since it is our species that has developed the capacity to dramatically change, for better or worse, its own course without waiting on evolution. No other creature has ever imagined a possibility as optimistic as democracy or as devastating as a nuclear explosion, let alone bring them to fruition. To have done so represents an extraordinary rebellion against our own history, cultures, and genes.

Without revolution and rebellion we would let mating and mutation do their thing. Instead, regularly dissatisfied with our condition, our body, our home, and our government we overthrow genetics through application of imagination, dreams, ambition, skill, perseverance, and strength. Every new idea is an act of rebellion, every work of art, every stretch for something we couldn't do before, every question that begins "what if . . ."

Most rebellions don't produce revolutions. A revolution claims, often falsely, to have an known end; a rebellion needs only a known means. When, in the late '90s, college students rioted on some campuses, a dean remarked with bemusement, "There was no purpose in it; it was a rebellion without a cause." The dean didn't catch his own allusion, but I did, because James Dean's movie, *Rebel Without a Cause*, came out the year I graduated from high school.

In it, James Dean as Jim tried to explain the cause to his father:

> Dad, I said it was a matter of honor, remember? They called me chicken. You know, chicken? I had to go because if I didn't I'd never be able to face those kids again. I got in one of those cars, and Buzz, that — Buzz, one of those kids — he got in the other car, and we had to drive fast and then jump, see, before the car came to the end of the bluff, and I got out OK, and Buzz didn't and, uh, killed him . . . I can't — I can't keep it to myself anymore.

Jim wants to report the incident to the police but his parents try to discourage him:

MOTHER: Why should you be the only one involved?
FATHER: Far be it from me to tell you what to do . . .
MOTHER: Oh, are you going to preach? Do we have to listen to
a sermon now?
FATHER: Well, I'm only trying to tell him what you mean. You
can't be idealistic all your life, Jim.
JIM: Except to yourself.
FATHER: Nobody thanks you for sticking your neck out.
JIM: Except — except to yourself.

In truth, Jim actually had a cause, a desperate, distorted, adolescent search for identity and honor in a society and family that seemed indifferent to such matters. Rejecting his condition was a necessary manifestation of his rebellion, but not its purpose. Those in power — deans, parents, media, or politicians — too often mistake the conflict for the cause.

A decade earlier, Humphrey Bogart, as Rick in *Casablanca*, faced some of the same problems but in an infinitely more sophisticated manner. He was all that James Dean wasn't. With skill and cool, Rick knew how to adapt to the chaos and deceit around him without betraying his own code.

Rick maintained his integrity and individuality by stealth even as others were using the same sort of deception to steal and destroy. The film's purist protagonist, the anti-fascist Victor Laszlo — is a noble prig next to the cynical Rick. "You know," he tells Rick, "it's very important I get out of Casablanca. It's my privilege to be one of the leaders of a great movement. Do you know what I've been doing? Do you know what it means to the work — to the lives of thousands and thousands of people? I'll be free to reach America and continue my work."

RICK: I'm not interested in politics. The problems of the world
are not in my department. I'm a saloon keeper.
LASZLO: My friends in the Underground tell me that you've got
quite a record. You ran guns to Ethiopia. You fought against the
Fascists in Spain.
RICK: What of it?
LASZLO: Isn't it strange that you always happen to be fighting on
the side of the underdog?
RICK: Yes, I found that a very expensive hobby too, but then I
never was much of a businessman . . .

Later Rick tells the beautiful Ilsa, "I'm not fighting for anything anymore except myself. I'm the only cause I'm interested in." Ilsa importunes Rick to help Laszlo escape, saying that otherwise he will die in Casablanca. "What of it?" asks Rick. "I'm gonna die in Casablanca. It's a good spot for it."

In fact, however, Rick helps to get Laszlo out of jail in time for a Lisbon-bound plane, shoots the infamous German Major Strasser, and watches as Ilsa leaves Casablanca in the fog with the handsome Laszlo — thus losing his woman but keeping his soul.

Rick is not a revolutionary, but is definitely a rebel. And he's not the only one in the movie, for as the gendarmes arrive following Strasser's death, the sly police official, Louis Renault, faces a choice of turning Rick in or protecting him. It is then, to audiences' repeated joy, that he instructs his men to "round up the usual suspects."

With *La Marseillaise* playing slowly in the background, Renault turns to Rick and says, "Well, Rick, you're not only a sentimentalist, but you've become a patriot." And Rick replies, "It seemed like a good time to start."

Of course, a well-schooled progressive of today might prefer, in place of such diffident heroics, the words of Mario Savio in 1964:

> There is a time when the operation of the machine becomes so odious, makes you so sick at heart, that you can't take part; you can't even passively take part, and you've got to put your bodies upon the gears and upon the wheels, upon the levers, upon all the apparatus, and you've got to make it stop. And you've got to indicate to the people who run it, to the people who own it, that unless you're free, the machine will be prevented from working at all.

Or some of the strategies recommended by Howard Zinn:

> A determined population can not only force a domestic ruler to flee the country, but can make a would-be occupier retreat, by the use of a formidable arsenal of tactics: boycotts and demon-strations, occupations and sit-ins, sit-down strikes and general strikes, obstruction and sabotage, refusal to pay taxes, rent strikes, refusal to cooperate, refusal to obey curfew orders or gag orders, refusal to pay fines, fasts and pray-ins, draft resistance, and civil disobedience of various kinds. . . . Thousands of such instances have changed the world but they are nearly absent from the history books.

In his own memoir, however, Zinn not only urges imagination, courage, and sacrifice, but patience as well, and tells a Bertolt Brecht fable with echoes of *Casablanca*:

> A man living alone answers a knock at the door. There stands Tyranny, armed and powerful, who asks, "Will you submit?"

The man does not reply. He steps aside. Tyranny enters and takes over. The man serves him for years. Then Tyranny mysteriously becomes sick from food poisoning. He dies. The man opens the door, gets rid of the body, comes back to the house, closes the door behind him, and says, firmly, "No."

There's also a bit of rebel in Raymond Chandler's private detectives:

> You don't get rich, you don't often have much fun. Sometimes you get beaten up or shot at or tossed into the jail house. Once in a long while you get dead. Every other month you decide to give it up and find some sensible occupation while you can still walk without shaking your head. Then the door buzzer rings and you open the inner door to the waiting room and there stands a new face with a new problem, a new load of grief, and a small piece of money.

Chandler says the detective must be "a man of honor . . . without thought of it, and certainly without saying it."

In such ways can rebellion be far quieter and more surreptitious than we suppose. For example, we tend to think of the 1950s as a time of unmitigated conformity, but in many ways the decade of the '60s was merely the mass movement of ideas that took root in the '50s. In beat culture, jazz, and the civil rights movement there had already been a stunning critique of, and rebellion against, the adjacent and the imposed.

Steven Watson credits the term "beat" to circus and carnival argot, later absorbed by the drug culture. "Beat" meant robbed or cheated as in a "beat deal." Herbert Huncke, who picked up the word from show business friends and spread it to the likes of William Burroughs, Allen Ginsberg, and Jack Kerouac, would say later that he never meant it to be elevating: "I meant beaten. The world against me."

Gregory Corso defined it this way, "By avoiding society you become separate from society and being separate from society is being beat." Kerouac, on the other hand, thought it involved "mystical detachment and relaxation of social and sexual tensions."

Inherent in all this was not only rebellion but a journey. "We were leaving confusion and nonsense behind and performing our one and noble function of the time, move," wrote Kerouac in *On the Road.*

It is instructive during a period in which even alienated progressives outfit themselves with mission and vision statements and speak the bureaucratic argot of their oppressors to revisit that under-missioned, under-visioned culture of what Norman Mailer called the "psychic outlaw" and "the rebel cell in our social body." What Ned Plotsky termed, "the draft dodgers of commercial civilization."

Unlike today's activists they lacked a plan; unlike those of the '60s they lacked anything to plan for; what substituted for utopia and organization was the freedom to think, to speak, to move at will in a culture that thought it had adequately taken care of all such matters. Although the beats are frequently parodied for their dress, sartorial nonconformity was actually more a matter of indifference rather than, as in the case of some of the more recently alienated, conscious style. They even wore ties from time to time. Yet so fixed was the stereotype that the caption of a 1950s AP photograph of habitués in front of Washington's Coffee 'n' Confusion Café described it as a place for bearded beatniks when not one person in the picture had a beard. Rather they were a bunch of young white guys with white shirts and short haircuts. Cool resided in a nonchalant, negligent nonconformity rather than in a considered counter style and counter symbolism.

To a far great degree than rebellions that followed, the beat culture created its message by being rather than doing, rejection rather than confrontation, sensibility rather than strategy, journeys instead of movements, words and music instead of acts, and informal communities rather than formal institutions.

For both the contemporaneous civil rights movement and the 1960s rebellion that followed, such a revolt by attitude seemed far from enough. Yet full-fledged uprisings can not occur without years of anger and hope being expressed in more individualistic and less disciplined ways, ways that may seem ineffective in retrospect yet serve as absolutely necessary scaffolding with which to build a powerful movement.

Besides, with the end of the Vietnam War, America soon found itself without a counterculture or — with a few exceptions — even a visible resistance by societal draft dodgers. The young — in the best of times the most reliable harbinger of hope; in the worst of times, the most dismal sign of futility — increasingly faced a culture that seemed impermeable and immutable. The establishment presented a stolid, unyielding, unthinking, unimaginative wall of bland certainty. It looked upon pain, aspiration and hope with indifference, and played out false and time-doomed fantasies to the mindless applause of its constituency.

The unalterable armies of the law became far more powerful and less forgiving. The price of careless or reckless rebellion became higher. Bohemia was bought and franchised. Even progressive organizations required a strategic plan, budget, and press kit before heading to the barricades. A school district in Maryland told its teachers not to include creativity or initiative in a student's grades because they were too hard to define. Hipness became a multinational industry and no one thought twice about putting a headline on the cover of a magazine "for men of color" that declared "The Rebirth of Cool," exemplified by 50 pages of fashions by mostly white designers.

One West Coast student told me bluntly that it was pointless to rebel because whatever one did would be commodified. Others chose not to confront the system but to undermine it in the small places where they lived. You would find them in classrooms or in little organizations, working in human scale on human problems in a human fashion. Their project was to simply recreate the human right where they were. They had implicitly rejected the nihilistic implications of the deconstructionism they met in college as well as the grandiose visions of previous generations. Such defined and manageable choices, particularly for the children of failed rebels, seemed the far wiser course.

There was something else: music. In rock and rap — as in blues and folk music earlier — people found that what they couldn't achieve could still be sung or shouted about. And central to this sound was not just the message but who was allowed to deliver it. For example, the music webzine, *Fast 'n' Bulbous*, described punk this way:

> Punk gives the message that no one has to be a genius to do it him/herself. Punk invented a whole new spectrum of do-it-yourself projects for a generation. Instead of waiting for the next big thing in music to be excited about, anyone with this new sense of autonomy can make it happen themselves by forming a band. Instead of depending on commercial media, from the big papers and television to *New Musical Express* and *Rolling Stone*, to tell them what to think, anyone can create a fanzine, paper, journal or comic book. With enough effort and cooperation they can even publish and distribute it. Kids were eventually able to start their own record labels too. Such personal empowerment leads to other possibilities in self-employment and activism.

To move from challenging record companies to taking on the World Trade Organization was not an easy or obvious journey, but clearly some of the attitudes that made the anti-globalization protests possible were formed in clubs and not at conferences. For example, Dewar MacLeod, writing in *American Quarterly*, observed that

> [Kurt] Cobain's death highlighted what the sociologist Simon Frith has identified as the central meaning of rock since at least the late sixties: true rock 'n' roll is supposed to be authentic, that is, anti-commercial and purely expressive. For some fans, this true rock 'n' roll can only be created through local, club-based, underground scenes apart from the mainstream productive apparatus of the multinational rock 'n' roll industry. From this perspective, the industry is the enemy against which the subcultural rock scenes define themselves, and like all of corporate consumer capitalism, the industry tries to co-opt the alternative

scenes, searching everywhere for more product. Once rock 'n' roll becomes merely product, its purity is threatened, as when Seattle's grunge scene burst through in the wake of Nirvana's success. The twin myths of "Rock 'n' roll Saved my Life," and "Rock 'n' roll Companies Stole my Scene" were the essential narratives governing Cobain's fame and death.

Lawrence Grossberg of the University of North Carolina told a seminar in the 1980s about some of the bumps in the road:

> U2, one of the more political bands to have become megastars, . . . played in my hometown (a Midwest state university town) to an audience of 25,000. At one point, Bono dedicated a song to Winnie Mandela; the applause which greeted this announcement was less than overwhelming . . . A group of students seated in front of me turned to ask if she was Bono's latest girlfriend . . . How is such ignorance to be reconciled with the band's passionate and explicit political concerns, and the fans' knowledge of both the music and the band?
>
> A few months later, Midnight Oil played to a smaller but equally enthusiastic audience. The response to the concert, and to Peter Garrett's stage performance, was overwhelmingly positive. But a common comment after the concert (and reiterated by the local music critic) demanded that the band "leave its politics at home." It's not that the politics were wrong but that they were out of place, irrelevant to the fans' experience of, and relationship to, the music.
>
> Finally, Fred Frith, an avant-garde rock musician who has had a respectable following in Champaign for some years, gave a concert there (to a few hundred fans, mostly undergraduates) the day after Reagan's second electoral victory. After the concert, at a party with many of his fans, he stopped the celebration (as only "star figures" can) to ask how many of his fans had voted for Reagan. He told me that he was quite shocked when approximately three-quarters of them responded positively.

By the end of the 1990s, however, an unremittingly political band, Rage Against the Machine, had sold more than seven million copies of its first two albums and its third, *The Battle of Los Angeles* (released on Election Day 1999), sold 450,000 copies its first week. Nine months later, there would be a live battle of Los Angeles as the police shut down a RATM concert at the Democratic Convention.

Throughout the 1990s, during a nadir of activism and an apex of greed, RATM both raised hell and made money.

In 1993 the band, appearing at Lollapalooza III in Philadelphia, stood naked on stage for 15 minutes without singing or playing a note in a protest against censorship.

In 1994, Rage organized a benefit concert "for the freedom of Leonard Peltier." In 1995 they gave one for Mumia Abu-Jamal.

In 1997, well before most college students were paying any attention to the issue, Rage's Tom Morello was arrested during a protest against sweatshop labor.

Throughout this period no members of the band were invited to discuss politics with Ted Koppel or Jim Lehrer. But a generation heard them anyway. And RATM T-shirts would become a common sight during the 1999 Seattle protest.

There is no good way to predict how such things will work out. Change often comes without a formal introduction. Like the time in early 1960 when four black college students sat down at a white-only Woolworth's lunch counter in Greensboro, NC. Within two weeks, there were sit-ins in 15 cities in five Southern states and within two months they had spread to 54 cities in nine states. By April the leaders of these protests had come together, heard a moving sermon by Martin Luther King Jr. and formed the Student Non-Violent Coordinating Committee. Four students did something and America changed. Even they, however, couldn't know what the result would be.

"You do not become a 'dissident' just because you decide one day to take up this most unusual career," Vaclav Havel would say while still a rebel. "You are thrown into it by your personal sense of responsibility, combined with a complex set of external circumstances. You are cast out of the existing structures and placed in a position of conflict with them. It begins as an attempt to do your work well, and ends with being branded an enemy of society . . .

"The dissident does not operate in the realm of genuine power at all. He is not seeking power. He has no desire for office and does not gather votes. He does not attempt to charm the public, he offers nothing and promises nothing. He can offer, if anything, only his own skin — and he offers it solely because he has no other way of affirming the truth he stands for. His actions simply articulate his dignity as a citizen, regardless of the cost."

◆ ◆ ◆

Not every revolt is just. One of Tom Stoppard's characters says, "Revolution is a trivial shift in the emphasis of suffering; the capacity for self-indulgence changes hands. But the world does not alter its shape or its course." Too often this is true. Infatuation with revolutions has been a particular handicap of the left causing such embarrassments as support for the Stalin regime when no possible excuse could be made for it. It is not that revolutions are wrong —

how can an American say that? Rather it is that, on average, revolutions are defined not by the wonder of their promise but by the horrors of what preceded them. They replace evil, but without a warranty.

To be a free thinker, Bertrand Russell said, a man must be free of two things: "the force of tradition, and the tyranny of his own passion." It is the obliteration of the former but subservience to the latter that creates the revolutionary dictator.

This is what James Thurber was telling us in his wonderful fable about the bear who had became addicted to fermented honey mead. He would "reel home at night, kick over the umbrella stand, knock down the bridge lamps, and ram his elbows through the windows. Then he would collapse on the floor and lie there until he went to sleep. His wife was greatly distressed and his children were very frightened." Then one day, he saw the error of his ways and became a fervent teetotaler. He would tell everyone who came to his house how awful drinking fermented honey mead was and he would boast about how strong and well he had become by giving it up. To prove this he would stand on his head and do cartwheels and kick over the umbrella stand, knock down the bridge lamps, and ram his elbows through the windows. Then he would lie down and go to sleep. "His wife was greatly distressed and his children were very frightened." The moral: "You might as well fall flat on your face as lean too far backward."

This is what happened to the officer in Vietnam who declared that it had been necessary to destroy a village in order to save it, and to NATO when it declared that Slobodan Milosevic's crimes against humanity were such that they justified the brutal destruction of a country and the very pain and death we said we sought to end.

In fact, every act in the face of wrong carries twin responsibilities: to end the evil and to avoid replacing it with another. This twin burden is analogous to what a doctor confronts when attempting to cure a disease. There is even a name for medical failure in such cases; the resulting illness is called iatrogenic — caused by the physician. In politics, however, we have been taught to believe that simply having good intentions and an evil foe are sufficient.

This is not true. Arguably from the moment we become aware of an evil, and certainly once we commence an intervention, we become a part of the story, and part of the good and evil. We are no longer the innocent bystander but a participant whose acts will either help or make things worse. Our intentions immediately become irrelevant; they are overwhelmed by our response to them.

Our language confuses this business terribly. That which is known at the personal level as terrorism is called humanitarian or a peacekeeping mission when carried out by the state. Thus both the office building destroyed by a few individuals and the country destroyed by a multinational alliance lie in ruins to support the tragic myth that Allah or democracy will be happier for it. But nothing grants us immunity from responsibility for our own acts. So if we are to revolt, rebel, avenge, or assuage, our duty is not only to the course we set but to what we leave in our wake.

◆ ◆ ◆

In 1997 Stephen Duncombe — academic, musician, and 'zine publisher — wrote a remarkable study of an American rebel subculture: *Notes From the Underground: Zines and the Politics of Alternative Culture*. In it he says:

> The powers that be do not sustain their legitimacy by convincing people that the current system is The Answer. That fiction would be too difficult to sustain in the face of so much evidence to the contrary. What they must do, and have done very effectively, is convince the mass of people that there is no alternative.

The 'zine publishing culture strips away that fiction, sometimes with brutal self-critique. From a 'zine called *Pathetic Life* and a writer named Doug: "You've got no money, no friends, you live in a slum, you never do anything interesting and you're too damn fat to have sex. Your life is pathetic." Says Duncombe:

> Marginalized people with little power over their status in the world still retain a powerful weapon: the interpretations they give to the circumstances and conditions that surround them, and the ideals and character traits they possess. Such is the case with zine writers. While there isn't much they can do about being losers in a society that rewards interests they don't share and strengths they don't have, they can redefine the value of being a loser, and turn a deficit into an asset.

Some of these publications, like the music of which they often write, are absorbed by nihilism. In this they are in a tradition that has led to good books and bad dictators, infamous philosophers and famous rock bands. Consider three comments about life, the first from Mike of the 'zine, *7 Aardvarks for Alice*:

> You sit there in your stinking little room thinking dire thoughts about your life that's so tough, and the society that represses, about your contemporaries with no clue, about your dead-end, mundane nine-to-five job, about your parents who never understood you anyway, and a government that encourages it all, and you get angry. You listen to avant garde music and read the fringes of mainstream literature. You dress differently and hate those who persecute you for doing so . . . Sometimes you write down these thoughts and mail them to others who basically

think the same things. Then you call it the underground. Then
you're dangerous, a true rebel . . . Bullshit.

The second is from a character Kierkegaard uses to parody the aesthetic men-
tality:

> I do not care for anything. I do not care to ride [a horse] for
> exercise is too violent. I do not care to walk, walking is too
> strenuous. I do not care to lie down, for I should either have to
> remain lying, and I do not care to do that, or I should have to
> get up again, and I do not care to do that either. Summa sum-
> marum: I do not care at all.

The third is from a song by the Ramones:

> I don't like Burger King
> I don't like anything
> And I'm against it

One of the problems with being so certain of what you don't like is that it
starts to define you. As Duncombe puts it, "the authentic self that zinesters
labor to assemble is often reliant upon the inauthentic culture from which they
are trying to flee."

A similar dichotomy arises when one consciously attempts to distance oneself
from the dominant culture in the name of individualism and freedom. Planet
Boy in North Dakota wrote to a 'zine in 1983 that he had defied local culture
by piercing his ears three times and coloring his hair, provoking this response
from John in the next issue:

> Punk is thinking for yourself and *being* yourself . . . Perhaps you
> don't realize it, but you are acting just like the phony society
> you're supposed to be against.

In the following issue, though, Mike wrote to say

> Who the fuck does John think he is? Some divine god who gets
> to call someone trendy for dyeing their hair and piercing their
> ears? Personally, I think it takes a lot of guts to look that wild
> and take all the shit people have to give.

Today, even in North Dakota, someone would have to do far more than
pierce his ears and dye his hair to declare freedom from society. Still,
Duncombe, who read a lot of such letters for his book, says that these debates

are really about something other than how one dresses or how one thinks. They are a debate about the "conflict between rebellious individualism and group identity." One philosophy professor raises this issue each fall by beginning his first lecture on individualism with a request that all those not wearing jeans to please rise.

A final disconnect found in the rebellion epitomized by 'zines is economic dependency on the despised culture. Without a multinational record and clothing industry, for example, youth countercultures would be far more isolated and diverse. The fact that the country's largest employer is a temp agency suggests that the economic setting in which today's young rebels find themselves is not entirely hostile. The bike messenger subculture happily serves society's citadels of conformity. And among the techniques used by the young to survive in expensive cities is "ganking," getting something at a discount or for free from a friend working within the system. One Washington ganker tells of a colleague who

> worked at a CD store and she let me use employee discounts to buy discs. Others, who worked at grocery stores, gave discounts on cartons of cigarettes, which we would later use as barter: in exchange for a free meal, we'd leave a carton on the table. . . . "It's a new form of Darwinism," says my friend Tessie. "The survival of the sneakiest."

And, of course, there is slack, defined in one manifesto as "like freedom but unlike freedom it brings no responsibilities." None of this is entirely new. The slacker has roots in African-American passive resistance against employers as well as in the crash pad culture of the '60s. As far back as the 1930s, a pair of critics attacked the bohemian as having "merely nullified for himself the necessity of accepting responsibilities upon whose recognition by others, however, he continues to rely for his privileges."

Of course, that sort of criticism comes most frequently from those without the impulse to rebel, not exactly the best vantage point from which to tell someone how to run an uprising.

◆ ◆ ◆

Far from such concerns can be found the government or corporate whistleblower. Typically a card-carrying member of mainstream culture, this defector is often but a reluctant dragon engorged with a sense of responsibility. Yet it is this most unpremeditated form of rebellion that can pay the highest price.

Whistleblowers, in the course of doing their jobs, typically stumble upon facts that point to danger, neglect, waste, or corruption. Far too often this discovery is met not with approbation and as a sign of exemplary public service, but rather as a threat to the agency or company. Among the consequences:

firing, reassignment, isolation, forced resignation, threats, referral to psychiatric treatment, public exposure of private life and other humiliations, being set up for failure, prosecution, elimination of one's job, blacklisting, or even death.

One such whistleblower, Pentagon official Peter Leitner, had his performance rating lowered, was kept out of meetings, harassed over sick leave, given a trumped-up letter of reprimand, accused of security violations, and threatened with charges of insubordination.

Jennifer Long, an IRS auditor, had a similar experience. She told the *New York Times*:

> They accused me of coming in late when I was at my desk an hour early every day. They instructed me to do something and then wrote me up for doing it. They wouldn't let me talk to anyone, they wouldn't even let me get out of my chair. I wasn't allowed to call my attorney. This went on for two years. They nearly killed me with the way they harassed me. But I knew that they would wear out before I did . . .

From the doctor in Ibsen's *Enemy of the People* to Karen Silkwood, the nuclear industry worker killed after her car was forced off the road on her way to talk to a reporter, speaking truth to power has proved costly. The Mongolians say that when you do it, you should keep one foot in the stirrup.

Whistleblowers fall easily into traps that can hurt if not destroy them. They may become monomaniacal, paranoiac, depressed, confused, and terribly lonely.

On the other hand, whistleblowers have forced the cancellation of a nuclear power plant that was 97% completed, potentially prevented widespread illness due to poor meat inspection, ended the beating of patients in a VA hospital, and exposed multi-billion dollar waste in the Star Wars program.

And not all whistleblowers are defeated. When Ernest Fitzgerald discovered a $2 billion cost overrun on a military cargo plane, Richard Nixon personally ordered his staff to "get rid of that son of a bitch." 25 years later Fitzgerald was still on the job.

Tom Devine, who works for the Government Accountability Project, has been helping whistleblowers for years. Part lawyer, part therapist, Devine presses his cases forward even as he tends to the personal stress of his clients. He has written a 175-page handbook, *The Whistleblower's Survival Guide*, to help government and corporate employees do what should be routine: tell the truth. At times he sounds more like a social worker than an attorney:

> To transcend the stress, it helps to be fully aware of and accept what you are getting into . . . The constant, negative pressure whistleblowers face can color your judgment and make you

paranoid about every event. Paranoia works in the bureaucracy's favor if it wants to paint you as an unreasonable, even unstable, person whose charges should not be taken seriously . . .

It is better to stay calm — and even to laugh — than it is to seethe with anger . . . It can be liberating to know that you have assumed responsibility for making your own decisions based on your values . . . Along with the pain and fear, there is real satisfaction inherent in taking control of your life . . .

Do not surrender to the temptation to become an obsessive 'true believer' in the importance of your whistleblowing cause.

Devine also warns his readers to expect retaliation and surveillance. One study found that 232 out of 233 whistleblowers reported suffering retaliation; others found reprisals in about 95% of cases. As Admiral Hyman Rickover told a group of Pentagon cost analysts: "If you must sin, sin against God, not against the bureaucracy. God may forgive you, but the bureaucracy never will."

◆ ◆ ◆

The rebel artist seeks to combine the freedom of the zinester with the whistleblower's dedication to a larger purpose. Art is the serendipity that occurs when imagination meets discipline and skill. Every work of art is a challenge to the status quo because it proposes to replace a part of it. An artist, therefore, is a rebel without even trying. Says printmaker Lou Stovall:

Art is by nature somewhat destructive. Every artist while seeking to add to the sum of art, attempts to take away your memory and appreciation of what went before, saying, "Look at me, I am new."

The artist is also free, perhaps the more obscure the artist the more free. As Virginia Woolf wrote, "Over the obscure man is poured the merciful suffusion of darkness. None knows where he goes or comes. He may seek the truth and speak it; he alone is free; he alone is truthful; he alone is at peace."

With acceptance comes all the little and big compromises that public reception demands. "Once you want something from them, they've got you," I.F. Stone warned journalists about their sources.

For most artists this problem remains only a blurry possibility. David Bayles and Ted Orland write that unlike earlier times when the artist was shored up by church, clan, ritual or tradition,

Today almost no one feels shored up. Today artwork does not emerge from a secure common ground: the bison on the wall is someone else's magic. Making art now means working the face of uncertainty; it means living with doubt and contradiction, doing something no one much cares whether you do, and for which there may be neither audience nor reward.

Then there are the personal fears: "I'm a phony, I have nothing worth saying, I'm not sure what I'm doing, Other people are better than I am. . . no one understands my work, no one likes my work, I'm no good."

In *Art and Fear*, Bayles and Orland address such concerns but still leave the reader with the unavoidable:

> Your materials are, in fact, one of the few elements of art making you can reasonably hope to control. As for everything else — well, conditions are never perfect, sufficient knowledge rarely at hand, key evidence always missing, and support notoriously fickle. All that you do will inevitably be flavored with uncertainty — uncertainty about what you have to say, about whether the materials are right, about whether the piece should be long or short, indeed about whether you'll ever be satisfied with anything you make.

And all this without wishing to change the world more than one picture's worth. Should your goal include not only creative work but political or social action out of that work, the uncertainties and problems compound. Does one favor the creation or the cause? Does one speak in the voice of the artist or of the leader?

For Stephen Duncombe it's a serial process: "Individuals can and will be radicalized through underground culture, but they will have to make the step to political action themselves. . . Culture may be one of the spaces where the struggle over ways of seeing, thinking, and being takes place, but it is not where this struggle ends."

Working in a period when it was hard to get a struggle even started, movement musician David Rovics felt compelled to write an open letter gently chiding his fellow activists for not using the arts more in their efforts:

> I have often been told by conference organizers that they have too many speakers for the weekend and no time for music . . . People organizing protests have often told me that the protest was meant to be a "serious event," thus music would be inappropriate . . . Often I've been told something like, "We're flying in Angela Davis and Howard Zinn and (fill-in-the-blank) to speak at our conference and we're also having a benefit concert, um, some local band, I can't remember their name . . . "

Perhaps some activists are driven solely by a sense of moral purpose and principle, and will persevere and never experience burn-out, but I've never met one like that. The most dedicated activists are people with human needs and desires, who require some kind of inspiration to continue their work . . .

Let us remember the words of the Wobbly minstrel, Joe Hill, who said, "A pamphlet, no matter how well-written, is read once and then thrown away — but a song lasts forever."

On the other hand, Bertolt Brecht, though a writer, feared that culture would turn out to be just an escape valve through which political tensions would be diffused without being confronted. Certainly we live in such a time of left-wing art and right-wing politics, of democratic dress and disappearing democracy, and of obsessive attachment to symbols over substance. Art in such a time can easily become a part of the problem.

But whether today's art is pro-apathetic or merely pre-political, functions and genres shift with time. Currently, the lack of a strong counterculture helps stifle political action, denying an outward and visible sign of inward changes. Ethnic and sexual literature has become personal instead of a Million Word March. And at the turning of the century, art was atomized and no one declared a collective renaissance of any sort.

But art is too unreliable to draw many conclusions from this. The silence may only have been the sound of something getting ready to happen.

Witness

Whether you call it God or Nature, argued Thor Heyerdahl, "the disagreement is about the spelling of a word." Unfortunately, a great many people have died in the name of correct orthography. In fact, many religions now considered benign long had characteristics we ascribe to "hate groups" — extreme self-righteousness, certainty that everyone else was going to hell, and social (or worse) sanctions against the unbeliever. Hear, for example, what comfortable words Martin Luther had to say about Jews:

> If a Jew, not converted at heart, were to ask baptism at my hands, I would take him on to the bridge, tie a stone around his neck, and hurl him into the river; for these wretches are wont to make a jest of our religion.

In 1870 the Vatican Council was still declaring that

> We anathematize all who do not receive as sacred and canonical the books of Holy Scripture in their integrity, with all their parts . . .

That most politically and socially powerful strain of American thought — Calvinism — justified itself by declaring earthly success an outward and visible sign of inward grace, hardly a charitable theology for the poor and the weak. The Southern Baptists were formed in the mid-19th century by whites demanding the right to own slaves. Only in the 1990s did the denomination formally apologize and begin to think about having multi-ethnic congregations.

Even today, anomalies remain. As recently as 1998 the Catholic Church anathematized all who believed in salvation by faith alone, i.e., the entire Christian fundamentalist population, no small group to disparage.

In this country, problems of religion and the individual have been with us since well before the founding of the republic. The idea of tolerance got its first real toehold in the mid-17th century colony of Rhode Island thanks to Roger Williams, who was a fundamentalist far to the right of, say, Jerry Falwell. Tolerance to Williams meant simply that one could practice one's own religion without being punished by the state or by other sects. It did not mean turning religion into a theological conglomerate in which faiths were just so many barely distinguishable product lines. In fact he considered the Pope the anti-Christ and declared that Quakers were but a confused mixture of "Popery,

Armineasme, Socineanisme, Judaisme, &c." His virtue, however, was that, unlike many others of the time, he didn't want to hang them.

Much as some would like to believe that this country originally consisted of a bunch of Jeffersonians defending the rights of non-believers, agnostics, Jews, deists and the like, the truth of the matter is that religious intolerance was quite common. Right up to the Declaration of Independence, Baptist ministers were still being charged with disturbing the peace and imprisoned in Jefferson's own Virginia,. One prosecutor complained, "They cannot meet a man upon the road but they must ram a text of Scripture down his throat." The state even had an official religion until 1821 as did Massachusetts until 1833.

What that exceptional and atypical group of leaders who designed our government did well — and it was no mean feat — was to ameliorate contemporary and future competition between religions. What they did far less well was to end the tension between religion and the secular. The prevailing view of the time was not far from that of New York state judge James Kent. A man named Ruggles had been found guilty of drinking heavily at a tavern and then going outside and blaspheming God, Christ, and the Holy Spirit. Chancellor Kent, on hearing the appeal in 1811, upheld Ruggles' conviction on the grounds that "the people of this state, in common with the people of this country, profess the general doctrines of Christianity." He further argued that to revile "the religion professed by almost the whole community" is to act "inconsistent with the peace and safety of the state."

In 1848, Supreme Court Justice William Story explained that the First Amendment was not there to protect the non-religious but rather "to exclude all rivalry among Christian sects, and to prevent any national ecclesiastical establishment, which should give to a hierarchy the exclusive patronage of the national government."

Thus the Jeffersons, Paines, and Franklins were curve-busters on the matter of religious liberty. Thanks to their consummate political skill, however, the apostate and infidel, the Missouri Synod Lutheran, the Roman Catholic, the Jew, the Muslim, and the Revolutionary Church of What's Happening Now ended up with many of the protections of the Episcopalian and the Presbyterian.

This didn't mean, however, that we wouldn't keep on fighting many of the same battles. They remain, albeit more subtle and complex. A few years back, I had lunch with a white anthropology graduate student from a suburb of Minneapolis. She was the product of a conservative Christian college and an unabashed fundamentalist. Towards the end of the lunch the student told me that as her faith had become more conservative, her politics had become more radical. You mean more like those of Jesus, I suggested and she agreed. And on many other issues we agreed as well.

The following summer she was to get married in the church that she regularly attended. She was worried about the reaction of her relatives because they too were Christian conservatives from Minnesota but unlike their daughter had never been in a nearly all-black church before.

Such people often pass us by because they don't fit the mold of what we think the debate to be about. They spoil the simplicity of the struggle, force us to look beyond clichéd dichotomies and into hearts, away from rules and rhetoric and towards a vague tone, an elusive atmosphere, an unexpected smile or an irrelevant kindness that turns out not to be irrelevant at all. They make yes and no seem less important and give religion back its grace.

Today the theological provenance of those consorting at annual prayer breakfasts is happily overlooked. Ecumenism has smoothed the rough edges of faith so that ethnic and class prejudice now has a much harder time escaping under the cover of religiosity. There are exceptions to be sure; Muslims, atheists, gays, or doctors performing abortions are still considered worthy targets by some with excessive pride in their godliness, but we have come a long way from when the most powerful of the world went around singing "Onward Christian Soldiers, marching as to war" and meant it. Literally.

Contemporary adaptations have also dimmed the recollection of how long the church in the west stood in place of the individual. And made no bones about it. In fact, as recently as 1997, the Catholic church was still denouncing individualism. A Rome gathering of hundreds of church leaders from the Americas, convened by Pope John Paul II, heard a bishop attack the "heavy emphasis on the individual and his or her rights" which had "greatly eroded the concept of the common good and its ability to call people to something beyond themselves." Cardinal Adam Maida, Archbishop of Detroit, warned that "we in the North are constantly seduced by the false voice of freedom that calls for individual choice."

In fact, the pull of individualism, even in a conformist era, does remain strong. In 1996, 51% of Americans told pollsters that teaching children "to think for themselves" was the most important thing for a parent to do in preparing their offspring for life. 18% listed "to obey," and still smaller numbers favored "to work hard," and "to help others when they need help." Only 1% listed "to be well-liked or popular" as most important.

Nonetheless, within Western culture the idea that we should think for ourselves is, in historical terms, still a relatively novel one. While there were ancient prescient voices like the Florentine philosopher Pico della Mirandola who said that it is given to man "to have that which he chooses and to be that which he wills," more typical was the advice of St. Augustine: "Hands off yourself; try to build up yourself and you build a ruin."

Today it's quite a different matter. Here, for example, is a list of some religious choices currently only a click away at Yahoo.com:

African Religions, Afro-Caribbean Religions, Agnosticism, Atheism, Bahá'í Faith, Buddhism, Bön, Celticism, Christianity,

Cyberculture Religions, Deism, Ethical Culture, Fourth Way, Free Daism, Gnosis, Hare Krishna, Hinduism, Humanism, Ifa, International Raelian Movement, Islam, Jainism, Judaism, Meditation, Messianic Judaism, Mithraism, Monasticism, Mysticism, New Age, Paganism, Pantheism, Process, The, Santería, Satanism, Scientology, Seicho-No-Ie, Shamanism, Shinto, Sikhism, Spiritism, Spiritualism, Taoism, Tenrikyo, Unitarian-Universalism, Universal Life Church, ULC, Veda, Voodoo, Won, Yaohushua, and Zoroastrianism.

Yet despite such a cornucopia, religion's cruel side and painful personal association still leave many with an ambivalence, indifference, discomfort, or even anger towards any formal organization of the spirit. Some depart their church or synagogue before they leave their families. Some leave until they have taken their unassisted selves as far they can, and then return. Some no longer want a roof between themselves and their god. Others attack every intrusion of church upon state with almost religious fervor, holding in contempt Reinhold Niebuhr's view that one does not resolve such conflicts by doing away with the church.

As one neither particularly offended by, nor attracted to, formal religion, I find myself often trapped between opposing certitudes. In truth, this Seventh Day Agnostic has met as many religious individualists as I have met non-religious zealots and robots. In the manner of other communities, those of faith can either stifle or liberate.

Freedom floats as well. If you violated the conformity of the ancient church you might have found yourself branded a heretic or an apostate. Today, if you violate the rules of the secular culture you may find yourself branded a neurotic or dysfunctional. Not all churches are run by people in robes.

Nor are all moral choices made in church. It helps, in fact, to separate our moral decisions from religious form, not because they are mutually exclusive, but because it allows us to see morality out of costume. Thomas Mann wrote of the need for those who would be individuals to recognize the difference between morality and blessedness, which John Ralston Saul describes this way: "A man who depends upon blessedness is one who relies upon God and his representatives to define morality and to enforce it. He is a child of God — a ward who would not dream of claiming personal responsibility. The individual is more like a child who has grown up and left home."

If we opt for blessedness, becoming wards of someone else's certitude, there is always the risk that we will confirm Oscar Wilde's view that he had never met "anyone in whom the moral sense was dominant who was not heartless, cruel, vindictive, log-stupid, and entirely lacking in the smallest sense of humanity."

The great danger of morality has always been the hypocritical arrogance of the righteous, centuries of whom have failed to distinguish between sharing a vision with others and imposing it upon them. They have also failed to see in themselves many of the evils they so strongly condemn.

On the other hand, if we take moral concerns — whether within the context of formal religion or not — as part of our normal business, but only in modest and conscientious concert with others, and only as sinners helping each other along the way, then potentially obnoxious or oppressive parody can become gently productive instead.

Once you remove the rituals and rules, even sharply contrasting moral traditions can share common ground. This was what Kim Hays found in a study of three Quaker and three military boarding schools. Though three taught the ways of war and the others non-violence, Hays found that together

> They are self-consciously moral. . . . They are places where adults deliberately attempt to practice a certain way of life and teach adolescents to be certain kinds of people. . . . These are schools where moral socialization is the acknowledged goal rather than the hidden by-product of education.

There were differences other than the opposing curricula of war and peace, such as the source of moral authority being internal in the case of the Friends schools and external at the military academies. But none of these institutions practiced indoctrination. Rather they taught morality in the context of conflict and ambiguity. They also shared "a desire to live consistently and with integrity, in service to certain strongly felt truths; a willingness to make sacrifices; and a belief in the sacred nature of their responsibilities."

Among the common values of the six schools were

- ♦ A clear moral tradition and a full-time moral identity
- ♦ Specific virtues such as equality in one case and loyalty in the other
- ♦ An argumentative climate in which these issues were discussed daily

Hays rejects the idea that morality is a social straitjacket on individualism:

> It does not simply reproduce the rules of collective life, but instead attempts to reconcile the individual's desire for self-determination with the society's need for order. Far from being a simple set of requirements, morality offers individuals the means to understand the chance to choose freely what is right.

In order to accomplish this, however, one must keep talking, a great deal of which went on in both Friends and military classrooms. It is also, interestingly, what happens on the Internet — a daily discussion and debate on the values and politics of a society in which too many of its leaders have far too little to contribute. One of the most common complaints about the Net by the archaic media is that it lacks "gatekeepers" or "middlemen" of information, which is only to say it is a medium without a hierarchy, one in which individuals become responsible for their own morality. When an early Friend was asked whether it was true that in his religion there were no priests, he replied, "No, in our religion there is no laity." The Net is much the same.

◆ ◆ ◆

The basic tenets of Quakerism were well described by a Friends headmaster:

> Friends, of course, have no exclusive claim to those principles which inform our school, but out of Friends' faith and practice, with its belief that there is that of God in every one, flow simplicity, self-discipline, honesty, community responsibility, non-violent resolution of differences, and unreserved respect for every individual.

When I was a student at that school, I was already a rebel and so would say things like, "The trouble with Quakers is that they don't fight hard enough for their beliefs." I would only later come to realize that the Quaker influence was on a delayed-time fuse; it was not until I joined the "real" world that I found how unique even the flawed application of such principles had been.

It would take still longer for me to grasp part of the wisdom of the faith: an ability to stand outside of time. Quakerism exemplifies the power of choice because it prescribes personal witness as guided by conscience — regardless of the era in which we live or the circumstances in which we find ourselves. And the witness need not be verbal. The Quakers say "let your life speak," echoing St. Francis of Assisi's advice that one should preach the gospel at all times and "if necessary, use words."

There are about as many Quakers today in America as there were in the 18th century, around 100,000. Yet near the center of every great moment of American social and political change one finds members of the Society of Friends. Why? In part because they have been willing to fail year after year between those great moments. Because they have been willing in good times and bad — in the instructions of their early leader George Fox — "to walk cheerfully over the face of the earth answering that of God in every one."

Those who think history has left us helpless should recall the abolitionist of 1830, the feminist of 1870, the labor organizer of 1890, and the gay or lesbian writer of 1910. They, like us, did not get to choose their time in history but they, like us, did get to choose what they did with it.

Knowing what we know now about how it's turned out, would we have been abolitionists in 1830?

Knowing what we know now would we have joined feminist Lydia Maria Child who recognized she would not live to see women's suffrage, but said that when it happened, "I'll come and rap at the ballot box?"

In 1848, 300 people gathered at Seneca Falls, NY, for a seminal moment in the American women's movement. They recorded a long list of grievances including the lack of access to higher education, the professions, and the pulpit; the lack of equal pay for equal work; and the lack of property and child custody rights.

On November 2, 1920, 91-year-old Charlotte Woodward Pierce became the only signer of the Seneca Falls Declaration of Sentiments and Resolutions who had lived long enough to cast a ballot for president. Would we have attended that 1848 conference? Would we have bothered?

◆ ◆ ◆

Other religions also place a strong burden of responsibility on the individual. For example, Islam, notes one writer, "believes in the individual personality of man and holds everyone personally responsible and accountable to God." Which is not that different from the Babylonian Talmud: "A person is always liable for his action, whether awake or asleep." Rabbi Joseph Telushkin explains in *Jewish Wisdom*:

> According to Jewish law, a person who breaks another's property unintentionally, e.g. while sleepwalking, still is obligated to pay for the damage. If this seems unfair, consider the alternative: The victim would remain under-compensated for his loss.

On the other hand, Judaism doesn't require you to feel responsible for the entire world's problems nor to commit the odd Christian sin of supererogation — doing more good works than the Lord demands of you. Rabbi Yochanam ben Zakkai even suggested that "if there be a sapling in your hand when they say to you, 'Behold, the Messiah has come!' complete planting the sapling, and then go and welcome the Messiah."

Such a blend of individualism, pragmatism, and responsibility has been translated into a wealth of prescriptions for social behavior that have stood the test of time far better than, say, those of the Harvard Business School. In Exodus, for example, it advises, "You shall not wrong a stranger or oppress him for you were strangers in the land of Egypt. You shall not ill-treat any widow or orphan." Similarly, Prophet Mohammed declares, "He is not a believer who takes his fill while his neighbor starves."

For the non-orthodox of whatever religion, the struggle for individual space within their religion is often hard-won. For some Jews it began with a rebellion against the centuries-old plenary power of the rabbis. A part of the story is told by journalist Paul S. Green in his memoir, *From the Streets of Brooklyn to the War in Europe.* He notes that by the dawn of the 20th century

> Jewish youth in Poland grew more and more impatient with the narrow focus of their lives. They were determined to take part in the opportunities opening up around them — exciting new developments in science, the arts, in social relationships. This brought them into conflict with their parents and grandparents. In seeking a different way of life, they began to do the unthinkable — to reject the strict age-old Orthodoxy of their ancestors.

Out of this grew several new movements, one of which, Zionism, looked towards retrieving a Jewish nation. Others were socialist, ranging from hardcore Bolshevik to the Bund, which Green describes as

> An organization of free-thinking Jewish youth who wholeheartedly embraced Yiddish culture and a Yiddish life that completely rejected traditional religion. The Bundists believed that only a socialist government — evolutionary rather than revolutionary — could hope to bring together all peoples of whatever origin and outlaw racial and religious conflict, with all men becoming brothers, thereby bringing an end to anti-Semitism and pogroms.

And so we find, not too many years later, the New York City Jewish cigar-makers each contributing a small sum to hire a man to sit with them as they worked and read aloud the classic works of Yiddish literature. The leader of the New York cigar-makers, Samuel Gompers, would become the first president of the American Federation of Labor.

Green's own family joined the rebellion:

> In embracing the principles of free-thinking non-religious belief, my parents had made a profound break with the past. The generation gap with their own parents was unbelievably deep. They had been born and brought up in a world that brooked no deviation . . . They were turning their backs on the fearsome God of their forefathers who had ruled Jewish lives for thousands of years . . . They realized that maintaining their beliefs set them apart from the mainstream of Jewish life, but the fact that they were a small minority did not bother them.

They became part of a Jewish tradition that profoundly shaped the politics, social conscience, and cultural course of 20th century America. It helped to create the organizations, causes, and values that built this country's social democracy. While Protestants and Irish Catholics controlled the institutions of politics, the ideas of modern social democracy disproportionately came from native populists and immigrant socialists.

It is certainly impossible to imagine liberalism, the civil rights movement, or the Vietnam protests without the Jewish left. There is, in fact, no greater parable of the potential power of a conscious, conscientious minority than the influence of secular Jews on 20th century modern American politics.

Sadly, however, social and economic progress inevitably produced a dilution of passion for justice and change not just among Jews but within the entire post-liberal elite. Thus we would find a women's movement much louder in its defense of the corrupt Clintons than about the plight of sisters at the bottom of the economic pile. Conservative black economists would decry the moral debilitation of affirmative action but fail to defend those suffering because of the massive incarceration of young black males.

Economic progress calmed the sound of revolution and reform; in its stead we found the conservative Ben Stein speaking at a Jewish anti-abortion conference:

> I'll tell you how I knew beyond a shadow of a doubt that the Jewish position in America had changed dramatically . . . The wife of a very close friend of my father died a few weeks ago and they had the memorial service at the Chevy Chase Club. And there was a cantor with a yarmulke giving the service at the Chevy Chase Club. And I cannot describe to you how astonishing a turn of events this was.

The great 20th century social movements were successful enough to create their own old boy and girl networks, powerful enough to enter the Chevy Chase Club, and indifferent enough to ignore those left behind. The minority elites had joined the Yankee and the Southern aristocrat and the rest of God's frozen people to form the largest, most prosperous, and most narcissistic intelligentsia in our history. But as the best and brightest drove around town in their Range Rovers, who would speak for those who were still, in Bill Mauldin's phrase, fugitives from the law of averages? The work of witness remained.

◆ ◆ ◆

While Quakerism and Judaism are the religions in America that perhaps have most directly confronted the issues of individualism and communal responsibility, larger faiths have also produced their share of strongly committed individuals. For example, Gordon Peterson, a highly respected long-time news anchor in Washington, came out of a strict Worcester, Massachusetts, parochial background without any apparent loss of identity: "The Sisters of Mercy taught me how to pray, and that's a good thing. The Jesuit Fathers taught me how to challenge authority, and that's a good thing. And the Xaverian Brothers taught me how to take a punch — and that's a good thing, too."

There is also, right in the midst of highly centralized, conservative, and hierarchical Catholicism, a strong tradition of personal witness. The best known examples are radical priests and nuns opposing war or engaging in civil disobedience, but a *Los Angeles Times* poll in 1994 found that even among average American Catholic priests, nearly half believed that birth control was seldom or never wrong and even more approved of masturbation. A Georgetown University study in 2000 of 1,200 Catholics found that two-thirds supported legal abortions, six in ten endorsed capital punishment and half supported physician-assisted suicide — leaving only 15% of Catholics backing the official church position on all three subjects. Another survey a few years ago found that more than two-thirds of American Catholics said that their own conscience trumped that of the Pope.

The *New York Times*' Jennifer Egan found among Catholic seminarians a particular emphasis on personal choice and responsibility:

> Witnessing is crucial, say the seminarians, because the world is starving for the message they represent. And here lies the crux of their sense of mission, and the optimism that fuels it: the so-called freedoms of our secular and relativistic culture have not paid off, they insist; on the contrary they have created a dangerous and uninhibited world where families are ravaged by divorce, abortion, addiction and violence. "Someone who chooses something they know is destructive, that's not freedom — that's slavery," said [Brian] Bashista. "Freedom is knowing your choices and then choosing the truth."

A seminarian once asked Saul Alinsky how, as he made his way up the church hierarchy, he could retain his values. Alinsky said that was easy: just decide right now whether you wish to be a cardinal or a priest. One of the seminarians interviewed by Egan had another idea: he kept a folder in which he placed any cards and letters he received that described the impact he had on people's lives: "There may come a day when I say, 'Was this all worth it? What am I doing here? Has this made any difference to anybody?' And if I ever come to that, I'm going to open the folder on that day. And if I get to the end of my life without ever having opened it, that'd be awesome."

OTHERS

The problem has always been other people. Wrote James Baldwin, "The universe, which is not merely the stars and the moon and the planets, flowers, grass, and trees, but *other* people, has evolved no terms for your existence, has made no room for you . . ."

Which may be why Americans, freer than most, have stayed on the run. The native American was forced westward by the young escaping the limits of East Coast American villages established only a generation or two earlier by parents escaping the limits of European villages. From the start, whether invading Indian lands, seeking a whale, rafting with Huck Finn, easy riding with Peter Fonda, or next week in Cancun, there has been a strong American belief that happiness lies somewhere else.

And yet as we find freedom we also rediscover loneliness. As geographer Yi-Fu Tuan says, we require both shelter and venture. We need freedom and support, silence and cacophony, the vast and distant, but also the warm and near, a voyage and the harbor, the great adventure and the hobbit hole.

The iconography of our times gives little sense of this. Instead, the individual is treated as a self-sufficient, self-propelled vehicle moving across a background of other things, other places, and other people. When this is not the case, as in a heart-warming newspaper profile of a community engaged in some noble task, the story is often crafted with such syrupy, fable-like simplicity that it simply seems irrelevant to what we know.

Besides, our own experiences with community may evoke something from which we have fled — a fouled-up family, a stifling neighborhood, little economic opportunity, an oppressive religion — rather than that which we seek. We may have declared, either consciously or unconsciously, never to go through that again. And so we look for maximum freedom and decline to make the trade-offs — except, of course, when we are working, commuting, or buying those things that are supposed to make us free. In the end, ironically, we may find ourselves having mostly freed ourselves from *voluntary* associations. Those relationships, appointments, and activities required by our status, employment, or to pay for our totems of liberation, are not impeded at all by our declaration of independence; rather they sit there happily munching away at what we, with an increasing sense of nostalgia, call our "free" time.

And so, perhaps surreptitiously, perhaps with clumsy premeditation, we may find ourselves seeking community again. Sometimes it's as easy as a pick-up basketball game, sometimes it's as tenuous as sitting in the back row of a church for the first time since adolescence, sometimes it's as quirkily satisfying as a book club going camping and kayaking together.

David Grenier in the zine *Retrogression* described well the awkwardness of getting it started:

> There were other people who were there by themselves. When we sat down, there was a guy at the table next to us who was obviously listening in to our conversation, obviously alone and bored. I know nothing about him, he could have been the biggest jerk, or he could have been a really nice guy. He could have been nice but stupid or nice and really intelligent. The only way to find out would be to talk to him. Hell, he's bored and lonely, we're bored and lonely, why not start trying to build a community by reaching out to other people? If he turned out to be a jerk, you put up with him for a while then leave. If he turns out to be cool you hang out all night and maybe exchange numbers. But I couldn't figure out how. I couldn't think of what to say. I couldn't take that first step. How do you intrude on a stranger's thoughts to invite them to come over and sit with you when you don't have a hell of a lot to offer? How do you introduce yourself to someone without it coming off like you are hitting on them or trying to sell them a copy of *The Watchtower?* That situation played itself out a few more times that night. A goth girl sitting on the sidewalk by herself, a guy who kept walking past us four or five times, alone, obviously looking for something, but I could never reach out.

It was a lot easier when you didn't have to invent your community. The problem, of course, was that you didn't get to choose your own community either. It was defined for you. For example, David Hackett Fischer in *Albion's Seed* describes four distinct types of communities created by the early British settlers in America. For each trait or value — such as freedom — he found distinct variations even within this narrow cultural band.

For example, in Puritan New England, freedom was strictly ordered; the community set its limits and described its character. If you didn't like it, you had to take your freedom somewhere else. In Virginia, freedom was hegemonic, which is to say the more power you had the more liberty you had. If you were a cavalier, you had a lot, if you were a servant you had little, if you were a slave you had none. "How is it," wondered Samuel Johnson back in England, "that we hear the loudest yelps for liberty among the drivers of negroes?" And John Randolph, as though in answer, said, "I love liberty; I hate equality."

In the back country there was a live-and-let-live gestalt, libertarian we would come to call it, while in the middle Atlantic colonies there developed a form of reciprocal freedom in which it was assumed that one couldn't be free unless others were as well. Four distinct styles for something that certainly existed but still didn't have a name; it would not be until the early 19th century that Tocqueville coined the phrase *individualism*. But you didn't get to chose between them; your style of freedom came with the territory.

One of the virtues of our present situation is that while community may be harder to find, it is also far easier to create. You don't have to found a new colony or risk your life in the unmapped west. Today, for example, there is hardly a human characteristic, from sex to philosophy to illness, that has not established its own "community." Even the CIA claims to be part of an "intelligence community."

Anyone who has belonged to such a group knows the support it can provide. From lover to mass movement, we just don't want to be free all by ourselves. What we really want, I suspect, is the right to take it or leave it, to draw at will from the well of others — their presence, their traditions, their ideas, their love — and then to blend it with everything that it is already in us in a way that is peculiarly our own.

This, after all, is how art is formed — by communities of ideas. Not by a big bang, but by mixing the borrowed with bursts of virgin imagination. It has been suggested, for example, that the blue note in jazz stems from the mating of the European scale with the tonalities of Africa; certainly much of what we think as unique in jazz draws from various cultures and the music would be far poorer if it didn't. Even rejection of artistic tradition requires knowledge of the rejected, for one can not leave a room one hasn't visited.

◆ ◆ ◆

No one has ever accused me of excessive conformity, yet like so many my individualism was formed not in isolation but within powerful communities. These included caring communities such as a high school that saw something in me beyond the scared, wise-acre kid I saw in myself. My college radio station was a creative community that served as a refuge and a garden for a motley collection of dissidents, odd-balls, minorities, and free-thinkers. This unlikely assemblage managed to create fine programming while still honing the distinctive personalities of those involved.

In the Coast Guard, I found a community of common purpose. Ships and the ocean have their own rules about such things. "Of all the living creatures upon land and sea," wrote Joseph Conrad, "it is ships alone that cannot be taken in by barren pretenses, that will not put up with bad art from their masters." From such an imperative comes a community of the competent. Discipline in the Coast Guard was lax in most respects save one: results. We were, for example, handed down a motto from the old Life Saving Service that clearly defined the limits of our individualism: "You have to go out; you don't have to come back."

Later, in a Washington neighborhood, I found a geographic community that, among other things, accepted communal responsibility for its young. This had a subtle effect on our children for they had more than two adult models nearby. And the "mayor" of our street for more than a quarter of a century was an artist — from the most individualistic of trades, yet the creator of community as well as pictures.

Perhaps in my case it went back earlier than all that, as I was reminded while being interviewed about my writing on the Clinton scandals by another presidential critic, liberal journalist Philip Weiss. Weiss asked whether it didn't bother me to be mixed up with all the right-wingers who were also on Clinton's case. Without hesitation, I replied no, that I had come from a large family and was used to being around people who disagreed with me. As it turned out, both Weiss and I were third children of six-sibling families. We had learned early the essence of politics: who gets the window seat, when, and for how long. And we had also learned about the failings of those bigger and more powerful than ourselves, such as older siblings or presidents.

This coincidence caused me to wonder about some other journalistic critics of the president. I contacted Roger Morris (author of *Partners in Power*), Sally Denton (investigative journalist and wife of Morris), reporter Christopher Ruddy, and independent investigator Hugh Sprunt. With the exception of Morris, all came from families ranging from four (Sprunt and Denton) to 14 (Ruddy). Only Morris and Sprunt led their sibling pack. Ruddy was 12th born.

Not only did large families predominate, but we each had strong moral influences in our childhood. Ruddy, the son of an Irish police lieutenant, told me, "My parents were patriotic. They believed in the country, in values. Of course we [didn't] have much money and it was sort of stressed that money was not as important as doing the right thing."

One of Sally Denton's grandmothers was an early 20th century feminist and another of her free-thinking ancestors fled mid-19th century Utah just ahead of Mormon enforcers. Weiss's parents were anti-Vietnam War. Mine were New Dealers who had started an organic beef farm even before *Silent Spring*.

Roger Morris was strongly influenced by his grandmother in the Kansas City of the Pendergast machine: "Her view of the inner darkness of real American politics left me an indelible sense of the shallowness and disgrace of most or our public discourse, the fundamental immorality of both old parties, and an abiding sense of reformist outrage."

Hugh Sprunt, describing himself as "not a complete Randite," had gone to church regularly through high school. It counted as a class. All through high school, I went to Quaker meeting each week and it, too, counted as a class. While he was reading *Atlas Shrugged*, I was reading *Stride Towards Freedom* by Martin Luther King.

In short, rather than being a sinister ideological conspiracy, we formed a confederacy of the hopelessly independent — this despite having been raised in large families suffused with moral messages. Rather than emerging suppressed and defeated, these early communities had actually helped make us rebellious and independent enough to challenge the most powerful man in America.

Communities do things like that — things that individuals can't and things that institutions won't. From the friend who drives you home when you've had too much to drink, to farmers rebuilding a neighbor's barn after a tornado, people draw strength from others that is unavailable in isolation. And in the process, they become themselves.

Communities can also create men and women unafraid of life's natural variety, who do not hide behind the doors of homogenous happenings — like the Brazilian Archbishop Helder Pessoa Camara who once declared:

> The bishop belongs to all. Let no one be scandalized if I frequent those who are considered unworthy or sinful. Who is not a sinner? Let no one be alarmed if I am seen with compromised and dangerous people, on the left or the right. Let no one bind me to a group. My door, my heart, must open to everyone, absolutely everyone.

In the end, it is as much a matter of our perspective towards communities as the communities themselves. Emerson put it this way:

> It is easy in the world to live after the world's opinion; it is easy in solitude to live after our own; but the great man is he who in the midst of the crowd keeps with perfect sweetness the independence of solitude.

◆ ◆ ◆

The contemporary free market mythology has obscured a basic point about humans: while we may be isolated competitors at times, this is no wise the central nature of our character. Some sociobiologists argue that we are biologically coded to try to get along with other human beings in order to protect ourselves. Or at least our genes. As one scholar put it, an organism is just a gene's way of making another gene.

In *Cheating Monkeys and Citizen Bees*, Lee Dugatkin says that one thing scientists do not disagree about is whether humans are social creatures. "We are, period. We know of no cases throughout history where large numbers of humans have intentionally lived outside the fabric of *some kind of* society. . . . We are simply not designed, either physically or psychologically, to live as solitary creatures."

Economists tell us otherwise as they keep trying to convince us that God's ways are better revealed by the dollar bill rather than by other values. To test the point, however, simply ask an economist how big a factor voluntary activity and unpaid work are in the gross domestic product. The answer is not all. The cost of murder, oil spills, cancer, and divorce are all factored positively into the equation, but housework, driving kids to school, or caring for an aged parent are not. Progress, it is implicitly argued, consists only of that which can be measured by money.

Jonathan Rowe, who has written about the misapplication of economics, calls such accounting "a grueling cycle of indulgence and repentance, binge and purge. Yet each stage of this miserable experience, viewed through the pollyanic lens of economics, becomes growth and therefore good." Rowe also notes that if it takes a $200 billion advertising industry to maintain what economists quaintly call "demand," then "perhaps that demand isn't as urgent as conventional theory posits. Perhaps it's not even demand in any sane meaning of the word."

An increasing number of scholars are getting around to examining some of the less mercenary and macho aspects of life, such as why we help each other out so much. For example, Dr. James A. Shapiro of the University of Chicago, who has studied the behavior of single-cell bacteria, says

> I don't know of any organism that really lives in isolation. . . . I think we are moving away from the reductionist explanations of animal behavior based on the behavior of single cells in isolation. Now we're looking at organisms, even bacteria, as parts of networks, in which single cells constantly interact with the higher organisms of which they are components.

At beginning of the Reagan Administration, Robert Axelrod began computer studies of the classic game problem known as the "Prisoner's Dilemma." In its traditional form, this game sets up four possibilities for a pair of captured prisoners:

- Neither prisoner informs on the other and thus are rewarded for mutual cooperation.
- Player A informs on B, with A being set free and B getting the sucker's payoff.
- B informs on A, with the reverse result.
- Both inform on each other so both lose.

What makes this complicated is that A and B do not know what the other is going to do. In Axelrod's experiment, the choices given were whether to cooperate or defect based on a logical reward system. Further, Axelrod proposed numerous repetitions of the game to make it more like a real situation.

Axelrod ran a tournament, inviting game theorists around the world to participate in a computer exercise of 200 moves. As it turned out, the winning entry was also the simplest program, dubbed tit-for-tat. In it, the player cooperates on the first move and after that simply imitates the other player's move: cooperation for cooperation and defection for defection.

In fact, reciprocity and cooperation worked so well they resisted the pressure of more aggressive concepts. Said Axelrod in *The Evolution of Cooperation*, "A population of nice rules is the hardest type to invade because nice rules do so well with each other." He proposed several principles for successful cooperation even in an unfriendly environment:

> Don't be envious
> Don't be the first to defect
> Reciprocate both cooperation and defection
> Don't be too clever

Since then, sociobiologists and others have challenged some of Axelrod's ideas and transformed others into more complex concepts. Matt Ridley in *The Origins of Virtue* warns that there is a dark side to tit-for-tat. What happens, for example, if one party accidentally defects; then the other side defects in response; which brings yet another defection, and so on. This, notes Ridley, is what happens in a "tit-for-tat" killing spree brought on by a factional feud.

Further, tit-for-tat assumes that those involved continue to play the game. Says Ridley, "If people can recognize defectors, they can simply refuse to play games with them." This technique, dubbed "discriminating altruism," insures that everyone "is playing by the same rules." In some cases, this involves social ostracism of the defector; in others the cooperators remove themselves from the field of battle.

Dugatkin, for his part, suggests that a number of paths to cooperation used by animals are more complicated than simple tit-for-tat. There is the alarm cry that a single squirrel — at considerable risk — sends its colleagues so they can scurry safely away from an arriving hawk. If squirrels were as selfish, and happiness a much of the product of that selfishness, as some would have us believe, the squirrel would simply run to safety and let the rest fend for themselves.

But what if it isn't the squirrel that is selfish, but its genes? Dugatkin notes that sisters share about 50% of their genes. If you were to die on behalf of two of your sisters, genetically speaking that would be an even trade. If you saved three sisters, your gene pool would come out ahead. Your family would consider you a hero; neo-Darwinists would view you as having been doomed by your genes.

Then there is the reciprocal altruism of guppies. Approached by a predator, a pair of guppies may move out to examine the enemy, then return and seemingly warn others of the danger. The easiest thing to do, if you are a guppy, would be to hang back and let another guppy take the risk. But then the greater guppy community would face increased danger. Despite their tiny brains, guppies seem to have grasped the notion of tit-for-tat. Dugatkin writes:

> Each fish keeps track of what the other is doing when both go out to examine the predator. Should one fish lag a little behind, the other fish slows down and makes sure that the distance does not become too great. To top it off, guppies genuinely prefer to spend their time hanging around other guppies who cooperated with them during their danger-filled sorties, presumably to be in their vicinity again, should the situation arise once more!

Still another approach is the teamwork used by wild lions. Instead of chasing a gazelle by herself, a lioness will work with one or more others to trap and chase it. Finally, Dugatkin describes group altruism, exemplified by the ants of the Sonoran Desert whose egalitarian consumption of food is preceded by just one queen going out — at considerable risk to herself — to collect it. Why? Dugatkin explains:

> When considering any behavior, one must examine the effect the behavior has on the individual undertaking it and those around it. If the behavior is beneficial to all involved, no obstacles exist to its evolution. If the behavior has negative effects on all parties involved, then such behavior disappears very quickly.

Ridley has his own menagerie of cooperation. For example, there is the naked mole rat of East Africa who shares underground shelter with 70 to 80 other celibate worker rats and one giant queen. "Like termites or bees, mole-rat workers even risk their lives on behalf of their colonies, by, for instance, running to block a tunnel when a snake invades it."

Perhaps most amazing are the more than 45 species of small reef fish and shrimp that clean parasites attached to larger predators:

> The cleaners are often the same size and shape as the prey of the fish they clean, yet the cleaners dart in and out of the mouths of their clients, swim through their gills and generally dice with death. Not only are the cleaners unharmed, but the clients give careful and well understood signals when they had had enough and are about to move on; the cleaners react to these signals by leaving straight away.

Another appealing example of cooperation comes from Merl W. Boos, editor of *Agricultural Notes*, who explains why geese fly in formation and what happens when they don't:

* A goose gets 70% more flying range thanks to the uplift from the bird ahead.
* If a bird falls out of formation it feels the drag and resistance of trying to fly alone.
* When the lead goose gets tired it moves back and lets another goose give it a lift.
* The geese in back encourages the ones in front by honking.
* If a goose gets sick or is shot by a hunter, two geese will drop down with it to provide protection. They will remain until the goose recovers or dies and then they will join another formation or catch up with their own flock.

We, no less than the geese, are driven by cooperative imperatives we may not even credit. Such as writing a will that leaves our assets to our children — in some ways a gene-preserving scheme in the guise of selflessness. Writes Ridley:

> All human beings share . . . the taboo against selfishness. Selfishness is almost the definition of vice. Murder, theft, rape and fraud are considered crimes of great importance because they are selfish or spiteful acts that are committed for the benefit of the actor and the detriment of the victim. In contrast, virtue is, almost by definition, the greater good of the group. The conspicuously virtuous things we all praise — cooperation, altruism, generosity, sympathy, kindness, selflessness — are all unambiguously concerned with the welfare of others. This is not some parochial Western tradition. It is a bias shared by the whole species.

Out of the new interest in the genetic provenance of behavior has come considerable controversy. Some see in it the ghost of past infatuations with eugenics. Others, like Ridley, see the evidence supporting a happy middle ground between Hobbes' view of humans engaged in a pitiless struggle and Rousseau's romantic natural person, the noble savage.

Melvin Konner takes a far dimmer view of the selfish genes. Writing in *The American Prospect*, he argued that "in art and poetry the lion may lie down the lamb, but in evolution the lamb gets eaten." Since he realizes this may not sit well with his liberal readers, he attempts to draw a distinction between what *is* and what *ought to be*. He argues that nothing in the neo-Darwinist arguments had changed the way he voted because "I want to live in a decent society." And he cites the Constitution as the sort of document humans need to hold their genes in line, "an intricate, elegant device, a sociological invention for keeping human nature in check, while allowing the conflict that seethes in the human breast to leak out through various safety valves."

Thomas Paine, he says, felt the same way. The Constitution, Paine said, was produced to "restrain and regulate the wild impulse of power." And in *Federalist 51* it says, "If men were angels, no government would be needed."

Of course, it's easy to believe in neo-Darwinism if you've done well enough in life to get paid to teach, research, and write about it. After all, humans are the only species to have created complex systems for mimicking or countermanding whatever it is that evolution and our genes are up to. One of these systems is called "higher" education which, among other things, decides who becomes a sociobiologist.

Anthropologist Robin Fox suggests that genes and culture actually function like a feedback loop. In order to survive the changing circumstances around them, humans took the cultural route; they simply had to move faster than evolution. But as cultural pressures grew, so did the natural selection pressures for better brains and "as better brains emerged, culture could take new leaps forward, thus in turn exerting more pressures."

In other words, a lot happens *after* we climb out of the gene pool and dry ourselves off. We are not like guppies or naked mole rats if for no other reason than that we can sit around arguing whether we are or not. Guppies and naked mole rats don't do that. What we think of as culture and history is really a form of artificial evolution. While both cooperation and selfishness have deep roots in our genetic core, nothing in this core made inevitable the Civil War or the end of small pox, Martin Luther King or Margaret Thatcher. Human choices did that, choices that included deciding what tools, virtues, bludgeons or trickery to pull out of the overstuffed closet of our humanness.

GUERRILLA DEMOCRACY

The ideal function of the American system is life, liberty, and the pursuit of happiness. Yet as we grope our way through our third century, the system in reality increasingly endangers human life, denies personal liberty, and represses individual happiness.

We live now with dishonest politics, disinformed and disinforming media, disconnected cultures, disjointed economics, dysfunctional communities and disrespected citizens. To attempt to repair such conditions without a morally conscious politics makes as much sense as trying to revive a body without a heart. This is not romanticism, idealism or naiveté, just basic political anatomy.

That we have come to accept a politics that offers no choice save between our acquisition of abusive power or our submission to it speaks only to the depths of our condition; it says nothing about that which is possible.

This condition has been largely the result of limits we have voluntarily accepted for ourselves. To those who would rule, manipulate, and lie to us, we have replied with remarkable apathy, repeated acquiescence, and utterly reliable consumption. These are precisely the responses that power seeks.

If we wish to change events there is no better place to start than to change our own reaction to them, to declare that a politics lacking justice, equity, decency, and compassion is no longer acceptable. Economics, efficiency, perception, and brutish power calculations no longer suffice. The bottom line has bottomed out.

The most radical act of individualism in which one can engage today is to come together with other individuals — as church, neighborhood, city, and organization — in order to uncover the biggest secret our leaders keep from us — that we are not alone.

We could ask the questions, raise the concerns, and share the ambivalences that might illuminate the way to a wiser and more just community. We could fill the air with the sound of voices not afraid to speak of decency and encourage those who profess to guide us — politicians, writers, academicians, and preachers — to join in our concerns rather than continue to lease their moral authority as though it were just another apartment on the market.

What would this look like? It might mean a coalition of conscience formed by the religious, by socially concerned business people, and by non-profit organizations to give the community a moral opinion on political questions and to set moral standards for politicians. It might mean a city or community coming together to discuss and discover common ground. It might mean academicians demonstrating their political conscience as well as their political facileness. It might mean children being taught once again what being a citizen and having a constitution is about. It might mean reporters treating ideas as news. It might mean a media more critical of the corrupt and less sarcastic about the idealistic. It might mean compiling indicators of a good and just society as well as those of a prosperous and efficient one. It might mean a country that asked *why* as often as it asked *when* and *how much*, and a culture that was concerned about the way something was done as well as what that something was. Finally, it might be a country that, just in time, paused to ask a question it had almost forgotten: what is the right, just, moral thing for us to do? And we might find that by just asking that question, we had already become a better people.

◆ ◆ ◆

Below the surface, things are happening. At a moment when both of the old parties are using increasingly disreputable means to reach their ends, there is a new politics of transformation arguing not only that the ends don't justify their means, but that the means help define the ends. You cannot, in short, have a decent society without a decent politics — a principle that Gandhi described as being the change that we wish to see.

Green thinker John Rensenbrink describes the politics of transformation as "a non-violent evolutionary method of seeking fundamental change. The change sought is in the direction of a consensus-building democracy, a community-based and ecologically sustainable economy and a person-centered social policy."

Such a social policy insists that the "freedom, mutual responsibility, and identities of all citizens are nurtured, respected, and celebrated." In Rensenbrink's view:

> Transformation can be conserving, reform-minded or revolutionary, depending on the context in which action is considered and taken. Transformation means reinvigorating citizens with a sense of personal worth and responsibility, it means reviving grass roots both in business and in government, it means choosing communities and the environment over the profits and power of mega-corporations and big government . . . Transformation requires both a sturdy defense of communities and persons and a resolute will to fundamentally alter the power structures of society at all levels.

This is a big order and one that not only breaks with elite political thought but goes well beyond that of traditional radical left politics. It also goes beyond conventional politics for its blends the political with the personal.

Says Rensenbrink, "The goal is not just to replace existing power with another power but to alter the way power is exercised." Political transformers, therefore, believe that not only must political power change, but the politician and the citizen as well — those exercising power and those affected by it. As in the decades before the American revolution — and during the civil rights, environmental, and women's movements — the catalytic legislative body must be the congress of our own hearts and minds.

One model for transformational politics is the Green political movement. Started in Germany in the early 1980s, the Green Party from the beginning intended to change not only what was done but how it was done. German Green Petra Kelly called the Greens an "anti-party party" that stood for "shared power" rather than "power over." In 1987, Kelly said, "Just repairing the existing system cannot be the solution for the Green parties. Our aim is non-violent transformation."

Not since the rise of the social welfare state has a political idea captured such rapid and far-flung interest. Today there are Green parties in more than 85 countries — without the direction of any centralized organization. It just happened, the way really important things often do.

Although ecological concerns are high on the agenda, the Greens are far more than simply an environmental party. For one thing, you can not get far into environmental issues without stumbling upon the rest of the world. You begin to see, in Kelly's words, that "there is a profound relationship between the fact that women and children are attacked, beaten and raped, and the fact that nuclear war and ecological catastrophe threaten our planet." And once you understand this, you begin to see that the inter-connectedness extends not only to apparently disparate phenomena but to the various strata at which they occur. Politics becomes no longer a simple matter of voting or debating "issues" but a pattern of personal habits and responsibilities. At this point, the antiseptic and puerile dichotomies of the talk shows, presidential campaigns, and think tanks start to seem vacuous at best, destructive at worst.

The transformational politics of the Greens stands in stark contrast to that of the two major American parties because it demands not only a central place for the individual but for the exercise of individual will and responsibility. In this it echoes both America's transcendentalists and Europe's existentialists. From the former comes the notion of ecological unity. As Emerson said, "the world globes itself in a drop of dew." From the latter comes a rejection of predestination and the concomitant need for people to form their own morality and then to act upon it. Together, they eschew false icons of authority, celebrate free will, and propose that we use it wisely. It is a far more difficult politics than one that is merely carried out on a trading floor where promises, like shares of stock, are exchanged for money. But it is infinitely more optimistic as well. In Kelly's words, with such a politics we can begin "fighting for hope."

What would a transformed society look like? It might be one in which we:

+ seek to be good stewards of our earth, good citizens of our country, good members of our communities, and good neighbors of those who share these places with us.
+ reject the immoderate tone of current politics, its appeal to hate and fear, its scorn for democracy, its preference for conflict over resolution, its servility to money and to those who possess it, and its deep indifference to the problems of ordinary Americans.
+ seek a cooperative commonwealth based on decency before profit, liberty before sterile order, justice before efficiency, happiness before uniformity, families before systems, communities before corporations, and people before institutions.

And it might be one that avoided what Gandhi called the "seven deadly social sins":

+ politics without principle
+ wealth without work
+ commerce without morality
+ pleasure without conscience
+ education without character
+ science without humanity
+ worship without sacrifice

◆ ◆ ◆

As during other moments of great tension, a spontaneous combustion of imagination has been occurring in places small and large as we discover how wrong we have been and how it doesn't have to be like that. The growth of innovative and cross-cultural spirituality, the ethic of voluntary simplicity, the rise of holistic medicine, the broad acceptance of ecological principles, the revival of college activism, and the transformational press have all been signs of a quiet storm building on the plains of the American soul.

This storm broke in the fall of 1999, leading to uprisings on campuses, in Seattle and Washington, and at the political conventions. The protests encompassed both specific complaints and a generic critique. Although the corporate media paid little attention, some of the most dramatic revolts occurred on scores of college campuses as students organized against sweatshops and on behalf of campus employees, attempting to force academia to live up to its lofty words.

Thousands of students independently decided to bother — to confront the immutable armies of the law. The reports came from all over:

CLAREMONT COLLEGE: Our bravest are still locked down in our administration building, and in need of support . . . It's alumni weekend so the fireworks are about to start crackin'. Those in the building are prepared to stay as long as needed. A recent survey of 136 workers found: 78% earn less than eight dollars an hour. 44% lack health coverage. 91% have no retirement benefits. 51% report managers who don't appreciate their work.

UNIVERSITY OF KENTUCKY: After a year of organizing, rallying and attempting to negotiate, the UK anti-sweatshop campaign came to a boiling point Tuesday at 5:15 PM when 18 students took over the basement of the Administration Building . . . The students, who had locked down with chains, PVC pipe, and bike locks, attempted to negotiate with the administration for eight hours. Over the course of that eight hours, students inside the building were subjected to intimidation and threats from the UK administration. "They were experts at singling us out one by one and intimidating us. They told us we wouldn't grad-uate. They told us we couldn't get accepted to the bar. They told us we would lose scholarships," said Lindsey Clouse, one of the students arrested at 1:45 AM Wednesday morning . . .

GRETCHEN LAKATOS, YALE: 30-40 people slept out last night and are sleeping out again tonight. We have erected an amazing structure that displays our demands, our arguments . . . We are sleeping out each night to defend our structure, so the admin-istration won't bulldoze it in the middle of the night . . . At Yale we have no student power at all . . . There was talk in the air of a joint student-worker-community governing board, real student power, academic diversity, etc. . . . We have realized that we need to tear down the walls of this ivory tower.

UNIVERSITY OF TORONTO: The eight remaining anti-sweatshop student activists holed up in University of Toronto president Robert Prichard's office survived a grueling weekend and they promise to remain until their demands are met . . . Lights are kept on at all times and the campus police have been blasting tunes into the occupied office almost non-stop over the weekend — pop songs during the night, heavy metal and thrash during the day.

JOHNS HOPKINS: Garland Hall has truly become our living room. Admissions, which used to use this space to welcome incoming students, moved out entirely on Monday, leaving us a swank desk and the entire floor space . . . There is not a wall without a poster, and we're beginning to collect posters from Baltimore and national organizations who support us, including a really swank banner from the Center for Poverty Solutions. I think most indicative of our support is the vast amount of food donations we've been getting. The big joke among protesters lately has been that "we can not be moved," thanks to donuts brought by the Black Student Union, snack foods brought by the All People's Congress, and our daily bagel-and-juice delivery from Professor Neil Hertz. Community members are also joining us overnight, and local high school students are mobilizing their schools with petitions, calls, and more. It may be a week and then some, but we're still rockin' . . .

The major anti-globalization protests that followed brought a reaction from police and government as brutal, anti-democratic and unconstitutional as has been seen in recent America. Dr. Richard DeAndrea reported from Seattle:

These rubber bullets took off part of a person's jaw, smashed teeth in their mouth. I saw the police arrest people who had their hands up in the air screaming "We are peacefully protesting" . . . I did see penetration wounds, I did see people bleeding. I did see teeth loss, I did see broken bones. There were children present, there were families present, they were firing upon families, mothers, grandmothers . . . We're treating people in a studio loft downtown. I just treated an ear wound. People have been treated for concussion injuries . . . Lots of tear gas injuries, lots of damage to corneas, lots of damage to the eyes and skins. They were using a pepper spray, a tear gas and they were also using some sort of nerve gas. We had reports of many demonstrators winding up with seizures the next day. It causes muscles to clamp up, muscle contractions, seizures . . . This shouldn't happen in America. This is still America, isn't it? I'm beginning to wonder.

The Washington demonstrations brought more of the same. Reported Augusta Gilman of the Independent Media Center:

We were not told until we entered the prison what charges were being made against us. The officers who cuffed us and led us onto the buses claimed they did not actually know what the charges were. Nor did the officers who guarded us for three hours on the buses. The commanding officer on my bus, who did not wear a name tag or badge, told us that the way the system was supposed to work was that if we believed we were being held against our rights, we could straighten that out in a lawsuit after our trial.

People on the buses with medical conditions were denied relief for hours. We were not read our rights, and were denied the possibility of speaking to a lawyer. When I was finally allowed my phone call, I was told that it could not last more than 30 seconds. There were too many people in line. I felt like a pig on its way to sausage, not a citizen on her way through the judicial system..

By the time of the GOP convention in Philadelphia, the government had dispensed with even the pretension of constitutional procedure. At the peak of the demonstrations, organizers reported:

- Officers dragging a man in the nude, grabbing a protester's penis, stepping on necks, jumping on a man's back, and slamming a face into a cell door.
- An officer who told a prisoner, "I'll fuck you up the ass and make you my bitch," slamming a man against a wall repeatedly, punching a prisoner in the stomach, holding a prisoner's face in the trash with his knee in the prisoner's neck, throwing a prisoner against the wall.
- Four cases of denial of access to medication: one person with HIV denied for two days, received on third day. One person with migraine, vomiting, denied all medicine. One hypoglycemic person denied access to adequate food.

A leader of the Ruckus Society was arrested while walking along a city street and charged with possession of an instrument of crime, obstruction of justice, obstructing a highway, failure to disperse, recklessly endangering another person and conspiracy. A judge set bail at $1 million. Joseph Rogers, a Quaker peace volunteer and President of the Mental Health Association of Southeast Pennsylvania, witnessed correctional officers tightening the handcuffs of protesters until their hands became blue. When Rogers asked the guards to loosen the cuffs, the guards replied, "This will teach them a lesson, this will teach them to come to Philly." Rogers was removed from his cell and cuffed from his left hand to his right ankle. "I told them I was diabetic but they threw me to the ground so they could cuff me. I was told to hop but my damaged knee prevented me. They dragged me to my cell."

Other arrestees reported being isolated, verbally abused, punched, kicked, thrown against walls, bloodied, and dragged naked across floors or through a "trash trough" containing refuse, spittle and urine. Said Paul Davis of ACT UP:

> I saw a man handcuffed to his cell door in a crucifixion posi-
> tion. He groaned and bellowed for 20 minutes that they were
> using metal handcuffs to smash his hands. I heard women
> screaming and being dragged along the floor. I saw a woman
> screaming in pain as a police officer said, "You want more?! You
> want more?!"

I cannot find in either my memory or in the modern record much that is close to the brutality and lawlessness exhibited by our government during these demonstrations. On other hand, seldom have so many so swiftly decided to become engaged — not merely to petition or stand in the street but to risk tear gas, rubber bullets, sordid imprisonment, and torture, and to be personally and politically transformed.

It wasn't just the young. One of the most remarkable events of the Washington demonstrations occurred with only one cop and a handful of media in attendance — as 700 steelworkers gave a warm standing ovation to the student activists in their midst. From the generational schisms of the 1960s to the hard-hatted Reagan-Democrat antipathies of the 1980s, it had become widely assumed that students and union members were the Serbs and Albanians of American politics. But the sweatshops abroad and the neo-robber barons at home took care of that — to the point that a burly George Becker, International President of the Steelworkers, could stand before his members and declare, "These are my sons and granddaughters. This is my family." And the members applauded.

"Every generation has to reestablish itself," said Becker. "Each generation is tested again and again on its resolve." Looking at the students in the hall, he remarked, "We know that when we pass the mantle, it will be in good hands."

Such a change from antipathy to apathy to the mobilization of melded con-science often happens in far more mundane ways than might be imagined. Even Martin Luther King hesitated when asked by sleeping car porter E. D. Nixon whether he would join what would become the Birmingham bus boycott. Nixon called King back a few days later, and the minister said he would help out. "That's good," said Nixon, "because we've scheduled a meeting in your church."

If you ask activists how they became involved, you often get answers like these:

- I wanted to know what it was about
- I was irritated about the issues
- I didn't like what elected officials were doing

 ◆ I like to serve and help people
 ◆ I was asked to

Some activism has deeper but far from distant roots. Green activist Rob Hager recalls that "When I was young I used to read books about Thomas Jefferson and others . . . The concept of justice came to have meaning to me, as much an art form as music or film."

Ellen Thomas, who has helped maintain a continuous round-the clock White House vigil for global nuclear disarmament since 1981, remembers the movie *Gandhi* and *The Day After* as influencing her. Also the songs of the Beatles, Joan Baez, and Pink Floyd. "For most of my young adulthood I was raising children in places where most people thought I was slightly demented because I wasn't happy with the way the world works." Then she took part in a demonstration that "changed my life completely; I gave up my job and joined a vigil."

Michele Colburn recalls:

> I was married for 15 years and was not politically active and was miserable, that's the only way I can describe it. I was critical of the way things were going, but not standing up for my beliefs. In short I was depressed because I was not "walking the talk" . . . I had outspoken and extremely liberal parents. I was lucky. They talked the talk, but I never saw them take action.

Mark David Richards, the son of evangelical missionaries, told me:

> At bottom, I have a feeling of justice and fair play that is imprinted in my consciousness . . . I think it in part comes from my parents' influence, seeing the way they put their heart into their work, building communities step by tiny step. But also from my country, which has told me about its ideals and its shortcomings. How could I defend my country if it couldn't even live up to its own ideals, at least most of the time?

Author Steven Shafarman recalls:

> My friends and I were collecting signatures on a petition one morning before school, with me stationed by the main entrance. The high school principal, who knew me, came over and asked what I was doing. When I showed him, he grabbed my collar and ushered me into his office. There he lectured me for several minutes about how "you should concentrate on

getting good grades. When you grow up, you'll understand that these other things are not so important." Without hesitating, I replied, "In that regard, I'll never grow up." After all these years, I'm still an activist.

Jan Levine Thal traces her activism to various sources:

> I don't exactly remember the first rally I attended, though I know its purpose was to oppose segregation. I was quite young but my parents thought it was important for me to know both that society was unfair and that it was our responsibility as white people of privilege (my father was an academic) to join in the fight to make the world a better place. They taught me not to cross picket lines and to abhor violence in every form. Our home was alive with protest and labor music; Paul Robeson and Woody Guthrie can still make me weep . . . I became increasingly convinced that the system fed itself on inequality and injustice not through error or poor judgment but because it was designed to be cruel for the many and profitable for the few . . . I stopped crying and became screamingly, blisteringly angry that a small group of rich white men consciously and determinedly benefit from the misery of so many. I became a Marxist, a Maoist, a feminist, a whatever-you-may and I'm still a little of each of those and more, but I found that to sustain a life of working for peace and justice I couldn't stay angry all the time. None of the belief systems I've encountered have helped me figure out how to live in harmony and happiness, with fun and laughter while still acknowledging and opposing the ruling class. I think Mr. Natural (a cartoon character invented by R. Crumb) said what I thought should be our anthem: "Hey kids, while you're out smashing the state keep a smile on your lips and a song in your hearts." I posted that in the bathroom of one organization I joined; I was roundly criticized for my petit-bourgeois attitude.

And so the brave, the exceptional, the engaged start out much like all the rest of us. They would have remained much like all of us were it not for a few experiences, a few words, a few songs that made them see life in a different way and want to do something about it. Saints, someone said, are just sinners who try harder.

Sometimes democracy's guerrillas take just a small piece of our disabled and distorted culture to revive — a school, a neighborhood, an untried idea, or some group of people the larger society has rejected. These activists will tell you they are not politicians, but in their very choice of community over institutions they have become another cell of transformational politics. And they instinctively accept the notion that John L. McKnight put well in a 1987 issue of *Social Policy*:

> The structure of institutions is a design established to create control of people. On the other hand, the structure of associations is the result of people acting through consent . . . You will know that you are in a community if you often hear laughter and singing. You will know you are in an institution, corporation, or bureaucracy if you hear the silence of long halls and reasoned meetings.

Here are some of the characteristics McKnight found among associations in contrast to institutions:

* Interdependency. "If the local newspaper closes, the garden club and the township meeting will each diminish as they lose a voice."
* Community is built around a recognition of fallibility rather than the ideal.
* Community groups are better at finding a place for everyone.
* Associations can respond quickly since they lack the bureaucracy of large institutions.
* Associations engage in non-hierarchical creativity.

Erich Fromm makes a similar distinction between irrational and rational authority, the former more often found in insitutions and the latter in associations:

IRRATIONAL AUTHORITY	RATIONAL AUTHORITY
Comes from power over people	Comes from competence
Based on fear	Doesn't need to intimidate
Exploits people	Doesn't exploit
Based on irrational awe	Based on rational grounds
Based on power	Based on performance
Is permanent	Is temporary
Criticism is forbidden	Requires scrutiny and criticism
Based on inequality	Based on equality

◆ ◆ ◆

Because of its belief in the importance of the *how* as well as the *what* one does, the politics of transformation throws up unexpected ideas, tests unexpected approaches and forms unexpected alliances.

There is nothing inexorable about ideological history. The Republicans were once the party of civil rights; Woodrow Wilson was a racist. Democrats have been both hawks and doves. New Deal labor voters became Reagan Democrats. Liberals ran from Joe McCarthy as a few conservatives stood up to him. Conservationists were once often political conservatives and today's advocates of organic farming span the political spectrum.

So one shouldn't really be too surprised, despite what we have been taught, if unexpected alliances develop, if new issues submerge old enmities, if new possibilities drown out old clichés. It doesn't mean we have turned to mush. It means, rather, changing circumstances and an acceptance of the true variety of human nature, of human history, and of the human spirit.

Traveling along the American political and cultural fault line I keep bumping up against anomalies — being forced to choose between abstract policy and specific decency, between the way it was and the way it is, between the matter that annoys us and the one that might kill us. It seems odd, yet it is right there in the midst of the anarchy, anger, ambivalence, and angst of unsettled America that one finds most strongly those traits of character, individuality, and stubbornness that got us through our first few centuries. It is messy, and it can be cruel, wrong, and dumb, but it has something that the talking heads, with their self-serving pleas for a "civil society" and their dainty rules of "public discourse," can not approach: the robust vigor of a democratic spirit trying honestly to find its way.

To survive in such a politics you must have set strongly one's own footings. The listless exchange of purloined bromides that often passes for debate will not suffice; nor will hiding in some safe corner with only the unalienated invited, nor speaking in sacred halls with supercilious sophistry. You have to know what you believe and not merely — as with the inner party of American culture — what you are meant to believe.

Such rooted beliefs and values need not be inconsistent with respect, friendliness or decent debate as long as we treat our beliefs and values as benign tools and not as weapons, as long as we seek to convince and not bully, as long as we claim only a fair share of the truth.

These are not, however, limits accepted by our leaders who daily rob us and then urge us to blame others; who speak of social harmony and build economic dissonance, who seek "one nation" while driving wedges between us.

We can, as those in charge would like, continue to define ourselves primarily by neatly described identities — either natural or acquired. We can remain interminably and ineffectually absorbed and angry about the particulars of infinite special injustices. Or we can ask what is it that makes our society seem so unfair to so many who are so different? If the young Hispanic in Watts and the militia member in Montana and the mother of six in Dorchester share untended miseries, might not those miseries share some common origins? Can we find universal stories in particular pain? If we can, it is the beginning of true change.

There is a lusty tradition in American politics of citizens of disparate sorts, places, and status coming together to put power back in its proper place. At such times, the divides of politics, the divisions of class, the contrasts of experience fade long enough to reassert the primacy of the individual over the state, democracy over oligopoly, fairness over exploitation, and community over institution. This could be such a time if we are willing to risk it, and one of the soundest way to start is to trade a few old shibboleths for a few new friends.

◆◆◆

But there is a problem. The system that envelopes us becomes normal by its mere mass, its ubiquitous messages, its sheer noise. Our society faces what William Burroughs called a biologic crisis — "like being dead and not knowing it."

The unwitting dead — universities, newspapers, publishing houses, institutes, councils, foundations, churches, political parties — reach out from the past to rule us with fetid paradigms from the bloodiest and most ecologically destructive century of human existence. What should be merely portraits on the wall of our memories run our lives still, like parents who retain perpetual hegemony over the souls of their children.

Yet even as we complain about and denounce the entropic culture in which we find ourselves, we are unable to bury it. We speak of a new age but make endless accommodations with the old. We are overpowered and afraid.

We find ourselves condoning things simply because not to do so means we would then have to — at unknown risk — truly challenge them.

To accept the full consequences of the degradation of the environment, the explosion of incarceration, the creeping militarization, the dismantling of democracy, the commodification of culture, the contempt for the real, the culture of impunity among the powerful and the zero tolerance towards the weak, requires a courage that seems beyond us. We do not know how to look honestly at the wreckage without an overwhelming sense of surrender; far easier to just keep dancing and hope someone else fixes it all.

Yet, in a perverse way, our predicament makes life simpler. We have clearly lost what we have lost. We can give up our futile efforts to preserve the illusion and turn our energies instead to the construction of a new time.

It is this willingness to walk away from the seductive power of the present that first divides the mere reformer from the rebel — the courage to emigrate from one's own ways in order to meet the future not as an entitlement but as a frontier.

How one does this can vary markedly, but one of the bad habits we have acquired from the bullies who now run the place is undue reliance on traditional political, legal and rhetorical tools. Politically active Americans have been taught that even at the risk of losing our planet and our democracy, we must go about it all in a rational manner, never raising our voice, never doing the unlikely or trying the improbable, let alone screaming for help.

We have lost much of what was gained in the 1960s and 1970s because we traded in our passion, our energy, our magic and our music for the rational, technocratic and media ways of our leaders. We will not overcome the current crisis solely with political logic. We need living rooms like those in which women once discovered they were not alone. The freedom schools of SNCC. The politics of the folk guitar. The plays of Vaclav Havel. The pain of James Baldwin. The laughter of Abbie Hoffman. The strategy of Gandhi and King. Unexpected gatherings and unpredicted coalitions. People coming together because they disagree on every subject save one: the need to preserve the human. Savage satire and gentle poetry. Boisterous revival and silent meditation. Grand assemblies and simple suppers.

Above all, we must understand that in leaving the toxic ways of the present we are healing ourselves, our places, and our planet. We rebel not as a last act of desperation but as a first act of creation.

HAT TRICK

H.L. Mencken once said that the liberation of the human mind has best been furthered by those who "heaved dead cats into sanctuaries and then went roistering down the highways of the world, proving . . . that doubt, after all, was safe — that the god in the sanctuary was a fraud."

Mencken made it sound easier than it is. It is a lifetime's work to clear away enough debris of fraudulent divinities, false premises, and fatuous fantasies to experience a *glasnost* of the soul, to strip away enough lies that have been painted on our minds, layer after layer, year after year, until we come to the bare walls of our being. Still, it is this exercise, however Sisyphean, that helps mightily to keep us human.

Inevitably such an effort initially produces not beauty or satisfaction, but merely a surface upon which we can work our will should we so choose, a barren façade empty of meaning, devoid of purpose, without rules or even clues to lead us forward. We stand before the wall as empty as it is.

It is at this moment that the deconstruction of mendacity and myth so often fail the social critic, cynic, and ironist — the street person overdosed on experience, the college graduate overdosed on explanations, the journalist overdosed on revelation. This is the point at which it is too easy to wash one's hands and consider the job done. Hasta la vista, baby, see you around the vortex of nothingness. . . .

The problem, of course, is that void. How people handle it can be drastically different. One may leave us with seven books, the other with seven dead bodies. In either case, we can not stare life straight in the eye without pain and without some longing for certainties that once spared us that pain. If we had been born in a time in which the therapy for doubt was punishment, even death, we would not be in such a fix. We would thank or fear whatever gods may be and go about our business if not happily at least with certitude. But the gift of decriminalized doubt changed all that. We are now free to be wrong by our own hand, to not know — worse, to have nothing and no one to blame.

That's why there are so many attempts to put the question marks safely back into the box, to recapture the illusion of security found in circumscribed knowledge, to shut down that fleeting moment of human existence in which at least some thought they could do the work of kings and gods, that glimpse of possibility we thought would be an endless future.

It is seductively attractive to return to certainty at whatever cost, to a time when one's every act carried its own explanation in the rules of the universe or of the system or of the village. From the Old Testament to neo-Nazism, humans have repeatedly found shelter in absolutes and there is nothing in our evolution to suggest we have lost the inclination, save during those extraordinary moments when a wanderer, a stranger, a rebel picks up some flotsam and says, "Hey, something's wrong here . . ." And those of us just standing around say, "You know, you've got something there." And we become truly human once more as we figure out for ourselves, and among ourselves, what to do about it.

No one seeks doubt, yet without it we become just one more coded creature moving through nature under perpetual instruction. Doubt is the price we pay for being able to think, play, pray and feel the way we wish, if, of course, we can decide what that is. Which is why freedom always has so many more questions than slavery. Which is why democracy is so noisy and messy and why love so often confounds us.

If we are not willing to surrender our freedom, then we must accept the hard work that holding on to it entails, including the nagging sense that we may not be doing it right; that we may not be rewarded even if we do it right; and that we will never know whether we have or not.

Further, the universe is indeed indifferent to our troubles. If God or nature refuse to cheer or punish us for our mercies or misdemeanors, the job is left up to us. We thus find ourselves with the awesome problem of being responsible for our own existence.

To make matters worse, we were set upon this task early in life with little hint that it even existed. The certainties of family, schools and religion typically protect us from the mystery while we are very young; we tend to learn about the loneliness of human existence about the same time we discover one of its few known remedies, someone else's body and love.

There is no discipline for doubt; no academy that addresses angst. We pretend it doesn't exist and then find ourselves seeking retroactive immunization from some guru of tranquility or therapy.

Given that we're talking about one of the central features of the human story, it seems a bit sloppy and strange to omit uncertainty from the curriculum, to not speak of how choice, informed by conscience and community, can give wisdom and direction to doubt. Or why it need not be the inevitable enemy of that triptych of human survival, the hat trick of integrity, rebellion and passion.

The subject matter is there; we just run from it. The cynic runs from the responsibility of replacing what has been destroyed and the convinced avoids the questions from the audience. Many of the rest are just afraid.

◆ ◆ ◆

There are exceptions, of course, among them those who view life in the manner of the existentialists. The history of existentialism is murky and confusing, for those lumped in the category have agreed on neither religion nor politics. But for the purposes of getting a life rather than obtaining tenure, Jean-

Paul Sartre's definition works pretty well. Sartre believed that existence precedes essence. We are what we do. This is the obverse of predestination and original sin with their presumption of an innate essence. Said Sartre, "Values rise from our actions as partridges do from the grass beneath our feet."

In fact, some existentialists argue that we are not fully us until we die because until that moment we are still making decisions and taking actions that define ourselves. Even the condemned person, one said, has a choice of how to approach the gallows.

Wrote Sartre: "Man is nothing else but that which he makes of himself. That is the first principle of existentialism . . . Man is condemned to be free . . . From the moment he is thrown into this world he is responsible for everything he does."

Sartre, while the father of modern existentialism, was not the first existentialist. For example, there was the theologian Kierkegaard, as conscious of God as Sartre was of Marx. According to Kierkegaard, writes Donald Palmer,

> We can never be certain that we have chosen "the right values."
> This means, among other things, that there is no such thing as existence without risk, and that existence at its very core must be experienced as anguish and dread by every sensitive soul.

To show just how murky existentialism can be, one of the most famous existentialist writers, Albert Camus, even denied he was one, telling one interviewer:

> No, I am not an existentialist. Sartre and I are always surprised to see our names linked. We have even thought of publishing a short statement in which the undersigned declare that they have nothing in common with each other and refuse to be held responsible for the debts they might respectively incur. . . .

Perhaps this antipathy stemmed in part from the fact that Camus was a novelist rather than a philosopher like Sartre, and perhaps because they disagreed on politics, but whatever you want to call it, few have spoken as wisely on behalf of the uncertain human spirit. "There is no love of life without despair of life," said Camus. "Accepting the absurdity of everything around us is one step, a necessary experience: it should not become a dead end. It arouses a revolt that can become fruitful."

These are not the precise and pedagogical words of a philosophy rising, yet, as with art and love, there is no particular reasons why life should be hostage to logical words, among the least fluid of human expressions. Robert Frost, asked to explain a poem, replied that if he could have said it better he would have written it differently. Louis Armstrong, asked for a definition of jazz, replied that if you have to ask, you'll never know. And, said Gertrude Stein, there ain't no answer. There never was an answer, there ain't going to be an answer. That's the answer.

In a world dominated by dichotomies, debate, definition and deconstruction, existentialism suggests not a result but a way, not a solution but an approach, not a goal but a far and misty horizon. It is, says Robert Solomon, "a sensibility . . . an attitude towards oneself, an attitude towards one's world, an attitude towards one's behavior."

And it's not just a heady matter of philosophy or religion. It spills over into business, personal relations and even politics. Mississippi writer Tom Lowe, for example, argues that, "The greatest evils in the world arise from two illusions:

> THE ILLUSION THAT "WE HAVE NO CHOICE." This belief manifests itself in various forms, the most prominent ones being the belief in the immutability (and often the depravity) of human nature and the almost religious belief in the justice and rightness of laissez-faire economic systems. This is ordinarily the illusion of the right. It is a flight from responsibility.
>
> THE ILLUSION THAT WE CAN PERFECT OURSELVES AND OUR SOCIETY. This is a corollary of the belief that people and their behavior are solely the product of their environment. This is ordinarily the illusion of the left. It is a flight from responsibility . . .
>
> The truth lies neither in the left or the right or in some middle-of-the-road position that borrows from both sides. The truth is that we are responsible for everything we do and for everyone and everything our behavior affects, and that responsibility extends to our collective, as well as our individual, behavior. Responsibility is like a seamless web — we are all connected with each other and ultimately with the entire world. It encompasses the choices we make in our capacity as spouses, as parents, as voters, as stockholders, as corporate officers, as employers, as public officials, and as purchasers of goods, but it extends to the entire planet.

This sense of being individually responsible yet part of a seamless web of others produces neither certainty nor excuses. One can, one must, be responsible without the comfort of being sure. Camus once admitted that he would be unwilling to die for his beliefs. He was asked why. "What if I'm wrong?" And when he spoke of rebellion he also spoke of moderation:

> There does exist for man, therefore, a way of acting and thinking which is possible on the level of moderation which he

belongs. Every undertaking that is more ambitious than this
proves to be contradictory. The absolute is not attained nor,
above all, created through history . . . Finally, it is those who
know how to rebel, at the appropriate moment, against history
who really advance its interests. . . . The words that reverberate
for us at the confines of this long adventure of rebellion are not
formulas of optimism, for which we have no possible use in the
extremities of our unhappiness, but words of courage and intelligence which, on the shores of the eternal seas, even have the
qualities of virtue.

Camus thus avoids the pedagogue's death by definition, preferring attitude
and values rather than direction. He would never have been caught, like that
pet of corporatist post-liberalism, Francis Fukuyama, writing a book called *The
End of History* and claiming that history "appears to be progressive and direc-
tional." While to the post-liberal globalist, history always proves the victor
right; Camus preferred to serve history's subjects rather than seek its spoils.

◆ ◆ ◆

Hectored, treated, advised, instructed, and compelled at every turn, history's
subjects may falter, lose heart, courage, or sense of direction. The larger society
is then quick to blame, to translate survival systems of the weak into pathologies, and to indict as neurotic clear recognition of the human condition.

The safest defense against this is apathy, ignorance, or surrender. Adopt any
of these strategies — don't care, don't know or don't do — and you will, in all
likelihood, be considered normal. The only problem is that you will miss out
on much of your life.

Another approach is to be lucky enough to live in a time of heroism. As
anthropologist Ernest Becker writes:

Men are naturally neurotic and always have been, but at some
times they have it easier than at others to mask their true condition. Men avoid clinical neurosis when they can trustingly live
their heroism in some kind of self-transcending dramas.
Modern man lives his contradictions for the worse, because the
modern condition is one in which convincing drama of heroic
apotheosis, of creative play, or of cultural illusion are in eclipse.

But even if we are not lucky enough to discover the West, fly to the moon,
or land on the beaches of Normandy, there are still some who write heroic
scripts for their ordinary lives, replacing the myths that society has smashed in
the name of reality. Says Becker:

The defeat of despair is not mainly an intellectual problem for an active organism, but a problem of self-stimulation via movement. Beyond a given point man is not helped by more "knowing," but only by living and doing in a partly self-forgetful way. As Goethe put it, we must plunge into experience and then reflect on the meaning of it. All reflection and no plunging drives us mad; all plunging and no reflection, and we are brutes.

It is from this well that is drawn the strength of good firefighters and good teachers and good grandmothers of children whose parents are no longer parents. Their lives are works of fiction written in order to survive the real, a reconstruction of the mythical support a society educated beyond its wisdom thinks it no longer needs. Instead of going to therapy, these writers of their own stories go about their business, preserving human lives as well as the human spirit.

The problem lies near our demand for rationality. As Becker points out, "What typifies the neurotic is that he 'knows' his situation vis-à-vis reality. He has no doubts; there is nothing you can say to sway him, to give hope or trust." And he cites G. K. Chesterton as having pointed out that the characteristics the modern mind prides itself on are precisely those of madness:

> Madmen are the greatest reasoners we know. . . . All their vital processes are shrunken into the mind. What is the one thing they lack that sane men possess? The ability to be careless, to disregard appearances, to relax and laugh at the world. . . . They can't do what religion has always asked: to believe in a justification of their lives that seems absurd.

◆ ◆ ◆

The existential spirit, its willingness to struggle in the dark to serve truth rather than power, to seek the hat trick of integrity, passion and rebellion, is peculiarly suited to our times. We need no more town meetings, no more expertise, no more public interest activists playing technocratic chess with government bureaucrats, no more changes in paragraph 32b of an ineffectual law, no more talking heads. Instead we need an uprising of the soul, that spirit which Aldous Huxley described as "irrelevant, irreverent, out of key with all that has gone before . . . Man's greatest strength is his capacity for irrelevance. In the midst of pestilences, wars and famines, he builds cathedrals; and a slave, he can think the irrelevant and unsuitable thought of a free man."

We need to think the unthinkable even when the possible is undoable, the ideal is unimaginable, when power overwhelms truth, when compulsion replaces choice. We need to lift our eyes from the bottom line unto the hills, from the screen to the sky, from the adjacent to the hazy horizon.

And nobody can do this but us. Hermann Hesse wrote, "Only within yourself exists that other reality for which you long. I can give you nothing that has
not already its being within yourself. I can throw open to you no picture gallery
but your own soul. All I can give you is the opportunity, the impulse, the key."
Emerson agreed, "Nothing is at last sacred but the integrity of your own mind.
Absolve you to yourself, and you shall have the suffrage of the world."

◆ ◆ ◆

There is so much to be done and so much fog around it. It is not surprising
that many in America have badly misread what has been happening. They continue to confront ideologies that no longer exit. They fail to see that those
leading both major parties march only under flags of convenience. They want
to discuss principles with those whose only principle is the pursuit of raw
power. They wish to discuss beliefs with those whose only belief is the defeat,
submission and ridicule of those who oppose them.

We are thus constantly being given false choices. The real choice is whether
we can achieve a future which, singly and together, we can experience as something other than an apocalyptic, angry, authoritarian era of violence, greed,
cruelty and planetary endangerment.

Once you reject such a future, the remaining choice is a commitment to
people, their places and the planet. It is the almost inevitable quality of this
decision — which each of us are already making either by intent or accident —
that suggests the particular power, hope and terrible danger of our times.

It is the choice of rejecting the internal logic of a technocratic system in favor
of judging things by their effects on justice, democracy, community and our
ecology. It is a matter of asking the right questions — seeking the right balance
rather than the best bottom line, determining human needs rather than institutional requirements, and finding the kindest and most sensible solution
rather than the quickest or most efficient. These are not just society's choices,
they are *ours*.

But here is the dilemma. It often appears, as Matthew Arnold put it, that we
are condemned to wander between two worlds — "one dead, the other powerless to be born."

How can one maintain hope, faith and energy in such an situation?

If we accept the apparently inevitable — that is, the future as marketed to
us by the media and our leaders — than we become merely the audience for
our own demise. Our society today teaches us in so many ways that matters
are preordained: you can't have a pay raise because it will cause inflation, you
are entitled to run the country because you went to Yale, you are shiftless
because you are poor; there is nothing you can do to change what you see on
TV. Campaign finance reform is hopeless. You may not act in a moral
fashion because you will look foolish; you may not take action because you

might offend someone; and you may not govern — you may only balance the budget.

And what if we follow this advice and these messages? If you and I do nothing, say nothing, risk nothing, then current trends will probably continue in which case we can expect over the next decade or so:

More corruption, a wealthier and more isolated upper class, more homelessness, increased militarization, a growth in censorship, less privacy, further loss of constitutional protections, a decline in the standard of living, fewer corporations owning more media, greatly increased traffic jams, more waits for services and entertainment, more illness from toxic chemicals, more influence by drug lords, more climatic instability, fewer beaches, more violence, more segregation, more propaganda, less responsive government, less power for legislatures, more for bureaucrats, less truth, less space, less democracy, less happiness. . . .

But what if, on the other hand, we recognize that the future of our society and our planet will in large part simply represent the aggregate of human choices made between now and then? Then we can stop being passive spectators and become actors — even more, we start to rewrite the play. We can become the hope we are looking for.

But we are not strong enough to be our own hope, you say. Then tell me how often has positive social or political change ever come about thanks to the beneficence, wisdom and imagination of those in power. Now tell me when it has come about thanks to the persistence of small, committed, weak groups of people willing to fail over long periods of time until that rare, wonderful moment when the dam of oppression, obstinacy and obtuseness finally cracks and those in power finally accept what the people have been saying all along.

John Adams described well the real nature of change. He wrote that the American Revolution "was effected before the war commenced. The Revolution was in the minds and hearts of the people . . . This radical change in the principles, opinions, sentiments and affections of the people was the real American Revolution."

The key to both a better future and our own continuous faith in one is the constant, conscious exercise of choice even in the face of absurdity, uncertainty and daunting odds. We are constantly led, coaxed and ordered away from such a practice. We are taught to respect power rather than conscience, the grand rather than the good, the acquisition rather than the discovery. The green glasses rather than our own unimpeded vision. Oz rather than Kansas.

Any effort on behalf of human or ecological justice and wisdom demands real courage rather than false optimism, and responsibility even in times of utter madness, even in times when decadence outpolls decency, even in times when responsibility itself is ridiculed as the archaic behavior of the weak and naive.

There is far more to this than personal witness. In fact, it is when we learn to share our witness with others — in politics, in music, in rebellion, in conversation, in love — that what starts as singular testimony can end in mass transformation. Here then is the real possibility: that we are building something important even if it remains invisible to us. And here then is the real story: that even without the hope that such a thing is really happening, there is nothing better for us to do than to act as if it is — or could be.

Here is an approach of no excuses, no spectators, with plenty of doubt, plenty of questions, plenty of dissatisfaction. But ultimately a philosophy of peace and even joy, because we will have thrown every inch and ounce of our being into what we are meant to be doing — which is to decide what we are meant to be doing. And then to walk cheerfully over the face of the earth doing it.

FURTHER READING
The following were particularly helpful in writing this book

Axelrod, Robert. *The Evolution of Cooperation.* New York: Basic Books, 1984.

Becker, Ernest. *The Denial of Death.* New York: Free Press, 1973.

Benedict, Ruth. *Patterns of Culture.* New York: Houghton Mifflin, 1934.

Bey, Hakim. *T. A. Z. The Temporary Autonomous Zone, Ontological Anarchy, Poetic Terrorism.* Brooklyn: Autonomedia.

Blonsky, Marshall. *American Mythologies.* New York & Oxford: Oxford University Press, 1992.

Brinton, Howard. *Quaker Journals: Varieties of Religious Experiences Among Friends.* Wallingford, PA: Pendle Hill Publications, 1972.

Camus, Albert. *Lyrical and Critical Essays.* New York: Alfred A. Knopf, Inc., 1968.

Camus, Albert. *The Myth of Sisyphus and Other Essays.* New York: Alfred A. Knopf, Inc., 1955.

Camus, Albert. *The Rebel.* New York: Alfred A. Knopf, Inc., 1960.

Camus, Albert. *Resistance, Rebellion, and Death.* New York: Alfred A. Knopf, Inc., 1968.

Chappell, Tom. *The Soul of a Business: Managing for Profit and the Common Good.* New York and Toronto, Bantam Books, 1993.

Duncombe, Stephen. *Notes from the Underground: Zines and the Politics of Alternative Culture,* New York, Verso, 1997.

Dugatkin, Lee. *Cheating Monkeys and Citizen Bees: The Nature of Cooperation in Animals and Humans.* New York: Free Press, 1999.

Eiseman, Fred B. *Bali: Sekala and Niskala: Essays on Religion, Ritual, and Art.* Boston: Tuttle Publishing, Periplus Editions, 1989

Fox, Robin. *Encounter with Anthropology.* News Brunswick and London: Transaction Publishers, 1991.

Grenier, David, *Retrogression Magazine: A Journal of Music and Revolution.* Seattle WA: http://davidgrenier.webblogger.com/.

Gross, Bertram. *Friendly Fascism: The New Face of Power in America.* Boston: South End Press, 1980.

Hays, Kim. *Practicing Virtues: Moral Traditions at Quaker and Military Boarding Schools.* Berkeley, Los Angeles & London: University of California Press, 1994.

Lager, Fred "Chico." *Ben & Jerry's: The Inside Scoop.* New York: Crown Trade Paperbacks, 1994.

Lowe, Tom. *The Jackson Progressive.* Jackson MS: http://www.jacksonprogressive.com.

McKnight, John. *The Careless Society: Community and Its Counterfeits.* New York: BasicBooks, 1995.

Morris, Brian. *Anthropology of the Self: The Individual in Cultural Perspective.* London and Boulder: Pluto Press, 1994.

Orwell, George, *1984.* New York: Harcourt Brace Jovanovich, 1949.

Palmer, Donald. *Kierkegaard for Beginners.* New York: Writers & Readers Publishing, 1996.

Ridley, Matt. *The Origins of Virtue: Human Instincts and the Evolution of Cooperation.* London, Penguin Books, 1996.

Rubenstein, Richard L. *The Cunning of History: The Holocaust and the American Future.* New York: Harper & Row, 1975.

Saul, John Ralston. *Voltaire's Bastards: The Dictatorship of Reason in the West.* New York: Free Press, 1992.

Shweder, Richard A. *Thinking Through Cultures: Expeditions in Cultural Psychology.* Cambridge: Harvard University Press, 1991.

Telushkin, Rabbi Joseph. *Jewish Wisdom.* New York: William Morrow & Company, 1994.

Watt, C. S. The Existentialists. http://www.tameri.com/csw/.

Wolin, Steven J. and Wolin, Sybil. *The Resilient Self: How Survivors of Troubled Families Rise Above Adversity.* New York: Villard Books, 1993.

Thanks to George LaRoche for his invaluable assistance.